More Praise for
Creating Training Videos

"If you've been looking for the best way to create a video for L&D, look no further. Jonathan Halls has a rare ability to translate complex, cutting-edge knowledge into actionable, transformative steps, and he's done it again here, combining his expertise in talent development and video production into a comprehensive, practical guide for turning your smartphone into a sophisticated development tool. You can become an expert at scripting, storyboarding, production, lighting, filming, editing, and countless other skills required to create a high-quality training video. This is a must-read book if you want to stay ahead in the L&D world."
—**Elaine Biech,** 2022 ISA Thought Leader; Author, *Washington Post* Bestseller *The Art and Science of Training*

"If you want a guide for designing, planning, and releasing professional quality videos made with your smartphone or other video-enabled device, this book is your answer. It provides clear, easy-to-understand, step-by-step instructions for creating engaging, instructional videos. The section with example screenshots alone is invaluable, not to mention all the other great tips, tricks, and techniques. *Creating Training Videos* won't turn you into Martin Scorsese or Francis Ford Coppola, but it will get you close enough to be the envy of your L&D colleagues and admired by learners who watch your videos."
—**Karl Kapp,** EdD, Professor of Instructional Design and Technology, Commonwealth University of Pennsylvania, Bloomsburg Campus

"*Creating Training Videos* is pure excellence! It's written in an easy-to-follow manner and useful for novices and pros looking for tips and suggestions to strengthen their training video creation toolbox."
—**Jay S. Naik,** Director, Training Center of Excellence, NYU Grossman School of Medicine

"This book is essential for anyone who wants to create effective, professional, and engaging training videos quickly with their smartphone. It's easy to read, well structured, and organised. Always keep it within reach as a handy reference."
—**Mhairi Campbell,** Journalist and Media Producer

"So you think you can make an instructional video? Not until you've read this book! Jonathan Halls shows you how to make one that actually works based on the science of learning. You'll learn how to capture your audience's attention and deliver important training that sticks with them. The book is packed with important tips that are easy to understand and, better yet, implement. It's a must read for anyone creating a training video, whether you have multimillion-dollar equipment or just a phone. I plan to implement his tips in my own classes."
—**Todd L. Belt,** PhD, Professor and Director, Political Management Master's Program, Graduate School of Political Management, George Washington University

JONATHAN HALLS

Creating Training Videos

Professional Quality With a Smartphone

atd
PRESS

Alexandria, VA

Photographs in Tables 6-1 and 6-3 and on pages 84–88, 111, 145, 146, 149, and 160–165 by Bey Bello. Figure 9-6 by lesslemon – stock.adobe.com.

ATD Press is an internationally renowned source of insightful and practical information on talent development, training, and professional development.

ATD Press
1640 King Street
Alexandria, VA 22314 USA

Ordering information: Books published by ATD Press can be purchased by visiting ATD's website at td.org/books or by calling 800.628.2783 or 703.683.8100.

Library of Congress Control Number: 2023948199

ISBN-10: 1-95394-696-8
ISBN-13: 978-1-953946-96-6
e-ISBN: 978-1-95394-697-3

ATD Press Editorial Staff
Director: Sarah Halgas
Manager: Melissa Jones
Content Manager, Learning Technologies: Alexandria Clapp
Developmental Editors: Alexandra Andrzejewski and Jack Harlow
Production Editor: Katy Wiley Stewts
Text and Cover Designer: Shirley E.M. Raybuck

Printed by BR Printers, San Jose, CA

Contents

Acknowledgments

This book took longer to write than you think—I began writing it at the beginning of 2023, but you could say that I actually started in the 1980s when I was a 16-year-old actor and made some low-key appearances on a TV soap opera. Watching the takes, seeing how camera operators lined up the shots, having makeup artists feather my forehead, and talking to the crew over lunch—that's when I started to learn about video. It's been a constant learning process since then, informed by all those who encouraged and mentored me over the years.

My skills and knowledge have been forged by so many incredible people who have taught me, influenced me, and taken me under their wing. While working at the BBC (where I led television, radio operations, and digital media training departments), my colleagues taught me so much about television production, especially the teams based at the Elstree Campus, where some of the world's finest television professionals learned single camera directing, production support, camera skills, and desktop editing. Not only did folks on these teams help me understand production at a depth I'd have learned nowhere else, but they also instilled in me a passion for the true spirit of video, which is all about pictures telling stories.

Here in the US, many folks have also been important in my development over the past few years. In 2011, Justin Brusino talked me into writing my first book on video for trainers (although it cost him some beers). Elaine Biech, who I jokingly call my therapist because I grumble to her about the training industry, is not only a good friend, but also a patient listener who is passionate about talent development. Courtney Vital collaborated with me to set up my first series of multimedia workshops in the US more than a decade ago, and in those early days, folks like Miranda and Alicia managed the workshop logistics like magic. There are also my mentors from 30 years ago—Alex and then Bruce—and the thousands of folks who've been in my workshops since 2012 and have helped me tailor my work to support their needs. And of course, there are the innovators you meet throughout this book whom I spotlight for the exciting ways they are using video to support talent development. All profoundly inspire me. Thank you.

I also want to thank Alexandria Clapp and Alexandra Andrzejewski for their work in the development phase of this book and for their insights both into what to include and how to package it. And I'd like to thank my good friend Jack Harlow (who has edited several of my books and still talks to me!) for picking up this project halfway through to see it to the end. Thanks also to Katy Stewts for seeing the book through production; Melissa Jones for proofreading; Shirley Raybuck for her design; Jes Thompson, John Higginbotham, and Farhad Farahmand for participating as models; and, of course, Bey Bello for his photography.

As important as all these folks have been, my biggest inspiration is my wife Sharon who encourages me in all I do, giving me space to be that weird thinker in the corner, and who with her smile each morning gives me a spring in my step.

When I worked at a radio station many years ago, my boss Bruce used to drop by my studio at the end of a morning shift. I anchored a current affairs radio program that was busy and tiring. He'd say with a grin, "It beats work!" Making media is not necessarily easy; in fact, it's hard work. But it's so much fun that it doesn't always feel like work. Have fun making training videos!

Jonathan Halls
Washington, DC

Introduction

Just about anyone can produce a video today. After all, most people carry a production studio around in their pocket or purse—their smartphone. But not everyone can produce video that looks professional and draws interest. And while some folks produce video that looks professional, fewer know how to create content that also provokes learning, which is what workplace learning professionals like you are called to do.

This book is for trainers, instructional designers, and learning experience professionals who don't want to produce boring stream-of-consciousness videos that learners quickly tune out. It's for folks who instead want to intentionally structure and craft content that helps learners build knowledge and skills for their work. Many trainers already create videos of varying degrees of quality but are thirsty for more formalized processes and principles of practice, while others may be starting to dabble in video production and want to know where to begin and how to save time making great content.

Video is the number 1 source of information for 66 percent of people, with more than 500 million watching Facebook videos every day (Adavelli 2023). And 90 percent of consumers watch video on their mobile devices (Shepherd 2023). When it comes to the most popular form of video that's consumed on the web, almost 30 percent watch how-to or educational videos (Oberlo n.d.). While this book isn't about marketing, many video usage statistics are generated by that industry. Nevertheless, interesting that 93 percent of businesses gain new customers through branded video content (Adavelli 2023).

Although many people watch videos on platforms such as Facebook, YouTube, Instagram, and TikTok, training videos have not been commonly used by talent development professionals for very long. In fact, my 2012 book, *Rapid Video Development for Trainers*, was the first (and since then, the only) published book for trainers on how to make training videos. Before 2012, training videos were almost always produced by professional film crews and production houses. Very few training professionals were making their own videos, and it was truly a pioneering time for video in the L&D space. Many organizations adopted techniques from that book, which were drawn from my experience working with companies that were adopting web videos as well as the core concepts I'd learned from amazing instructors while working at the BBC.

But a lot has changed since 2012. For example, back in those days, the videos produced by training departments were often done by IT folks, who understood editing software and how to tweak complex settings on their camera, or a person in the training department who was a photography enthusiast. And they were typically using the same standalone consumer model camera that they used to film their toddler's first steps. Designers and trainers who wanted a video for their class would ask these folks to make them. Today, trainers like you are producing your own videos, which is a good thing—you're putting yourself in the driver's seat to plan, film, and edit these videos, rather than ceding control to someone else. You're capturing terrific quality videos with the powerful camera embedded in your smartphone. Plus, through our colleagues' trailblazing efforts and new media research, we've learned a lot in the last decade about how video can support learning and talent development, which we cover thoroughly in this book.

In This Book

While videos are fun to make, they can be time consuming, especially when you're inexperienced. If you're new to making your own training videos, you should read this book from start to finish. However, if you're more experienced, you might prefer to dip in and out for specific aspects of planning, filming, and editing as necessary for your production. Accordingly, this book is divided into four parts:

1. **Video and learning.** I explore how video is being used in the L&D world, how learning happens and what it means for training videos, and key principles you can follow to ensure your videos provoke learning.

2. **Keeping eyeballs on your video.** I look at what makes video engaging. I draw on insights from TV and film, exploring visual grammar and how to plan your footage and structure videos to support learning.

3. **Tools of the trade.** This is the part of video production most people look at first. I cover the gear you need and how to use it so your shots look professional, editing software, key principles for professional editing, and good production practices. I take knowledge from the professional production world and apply it to L&D and new gear such as phones and tablets.

4. **Workflow and business processes.** No one has much time these days, so I discuss how to crank out training videos efficiently and avoid wasting time. My workshop attendees have told me that they struggle with managing stakeholders (like subject matter experts) and project management activities in production. I outline what you can do to make video production as much a part of your training team's practice as doing a needs assessment or planning a workshop.

People go to film school to learn good production techniques. Journalists spend years at J-school and then work as "cadets" to forge their skills. So, while I'm conscious that this book doesn't cover everything, I've decided to aim for breadth rather than depth. I've provided an overall framework so you can understand what you need to do to craft powerful training videos. Through practice and further reading, you'll improve your individual skills.

PART 1
VIDEO AND LEARNING

To get the most value out of video as an L&D tool, it's important to understand how video works as a modality, along with its strengths and weaknesses. You also need to know how learning happens so you can structure video content to be quick and easy to understand as well as easy to remember and put into practice.

In this part of the book, I look at why videos are important and how you can use them. Then, I take a whistle-stop tour of the learning process and consider what it means for video. I also explore video as a communication modality, which leads into a conversation about how to optimize learning and video.

Chapter 1
The Case for Video

In this chapter, you'll learn about:
- How video helps trainers, coaches, and educators
- How trainers are using video
- Video narrative formats
- Selling video to your boss

Video enables learning and talent development professionals to be more agile, reach more people, and meet their training needs, both bringing the world of work into the classroom and taking learning beyond the classroom walls to be accessed when needed. It also solves some traditional instruction challenges, whether synchronous or asynchronous.

Making Learning Relevant and Real

One of the challenges of any training program is making content relevant and real. How do you effectively help learners understand the size and motion of a turbine without taking them on-site? How do you get learners close to a ship's propellor without having them don scuba suits and take the potentially dangerous dive below a large ship? How do you show aircraft mechanics how first-class seats are bolted into the first-class cabin without taking an aircraft out of service to bring learners onboard? In many situations, these topics are taught by showing learners diagrams on PowerPoint slides, which can feel far removed from reality. However, video can take learners directly to the place where a task is performed, capturing its real size and scope.

The cost of taking an aircraft out of action for training is huge, and if you need to do it for multiple training cohorts, those costs add up, especially if each cohort needs to access the equipment multiple times. Before long, the finance department will call the chief learning officer to ask if the expense of taking an aircraft out of flying is necessary. However, if you take the aircraft out of commission once and film a demonstration of how each component bolts together, you can create a virtual field trip that saves money in the long term. It doesn't mean mechanics will never go onboard to practice their skills; it just means that the time the aircraft is not flying is minimized.

If you're teaching soft skills, like nonverbal communication, video can provide huge value. These courses often involve someone doing double duty as both trainer and actor as they demonstrate key actions. Perhaps they ask a participant to demonstrate body language. In some cases, another trainer might join the class for an hour to demonstrate key actions, which then takes them from their course or other activities like coaching. However, you can hire some actors (or use the trainers) once and film them. Then, the video can be used multiple times, freeing up resources.

Bringing the Real World Into the Learning Experience

Video allows trainers to bring the outside world into the classroom and save money while doing it. Video also enables trainers to orchestrate demonstrations and virtual field trips with precision to minimize awkward moments. What happens if you drop the wrench or screwdriver when showing people how to pull apart a first-class airplane seat? Well, simply pick it up, start again, and edit out the dropped wrench. Who wants to set everything up for a second demo after the first one went wrong? The video will show a key learning moment done right and reduce cognitive load by avoiding mistakes and other distractions.

Another challenge in corporate training involves inviting subject matter experts (SMEs) into the classroom. They bring up-to-date expertise and gritty stories that reflect the real world of work and add authenticity to learning experiences. Whether the SME is a psychologist explaining nuances in conflict resolution, a forensic accountant sharing new ways to uncover data, or a key team member sharing workplace culture tips for new employees during onboarding, video can bring their expertise directly to learners in a classroom.

A few years ago, I worked with a client who found enormous value in incorporating SMEs and experienced staff into their onboarding program. The new recruits loved hearing honest and sometimes humorous descriptions of the real work they were about to engage in. One of the guest SMEs in particular had an inane sense of humor—while highlighting key things folks needed to learn, she also left them in stitches. The training department did everything they could to have her as a guest in the onboarding class because she got new employees excited about their jobs. However, after three months and a lot of time away from her desk, her boss told the trainers that such cameos were not sustainable, and they lost a key SME. My team remedied that with video. But the video didn't just bring back a popular presenter. We were able to make her presentation more engaging with cutaways to locations and objects she was talking about, giving it greater authenticity and better preparing new staff for their work.

Taking Learning Into the World Where and When Needed

Video doesn't just bring the world into the classroom; it also takes the classroom into the world because it's the ideal modality for crafting learning into packages that are easily accessed in the field when they're needed. For example, if a supermarket technician needs to fix an automatic teller in store, they can watch a short on-demand video with step-by-step instructions and close-ups of relevant components and fix it on the spot.

Training videos can radically transform the learning experience, making it more learner centric. The traditional classroom experience, whether physical or virtual, is generally scheduled ahead of time. That schedule is determined by when a classroom is available (for a physical class), when a producer is available (for a virtual class), and when the trainer or SME is available. Because it's easier to schedule trainers and producers in chunks of time like a day or half-day, rather than on an hourly basis, courses are usually packaged into a half day or a couple days when the room, trainer, and, for virtual learning, the producer is available. It doesn't matter whether it's convenient for the learner or if a series of shorter classes would be better for their learning because it comes down to available resources. Learners across the organization must fit their schedule around the trainer's. This isn't learner centered—an important principle our profession holds—simply because there are too many moving parts to consider.

The complexity of scheduling isn't the only dynamic that can undermine your ability to facilitate learner-centric training. Instructional designers and trainers are now bound by their scheduled time with learners. Rather than design experiences around the topic, the content is squeezed into a day. For example, one task may only need 45 minutes of instruction followed by a day or two of practice. But, if the trainer is available for whole or half day intervals, they will squeeze more content into the half day to make the most of the time. When else will they get that time with the participants? Their learners will leave the half-day class having been taught multiple topics or tasks that they will promptly forget. Or perhaps a task takes four hours to learn, but the trainer must compress the content into a three-and-a-half-hour window. Now they're designing the learning experience to suit the time, not the topic or learner. Videos allow you to craft on-demand learning experiences for each task so the employee can access when needed. No longer must the learner sit through a half-day webinar watching five tasks they'll quickly forget. Now they can watch a short video of a single task when needed.

I've been talking about learning in the context of an L&D experience, but, if you take a step back and look at how learning happens in real life, it's much more flexible. At home, when I need to learn how to brine chicken, I pull up a video on YouTube. If I need to know how to use a router in my home workshop, I watch a video hosted by *This Old House*. It's a modern way of thinking about learning. Of course, learning outside the organization is more organic and self-directed. Can the same be true for the L&D experience? If you're a SME with an online course, using video to show tasks or key content can give you the opportunity to provide the needed content at the right time with the option for learners to direct their learning path.

The State of Instructional Video

In 2021, the Learning Guild conducted research into how video is used in today's organizations and asked me to review and write its bi-annual report. While the findings may not have been groundbreaking, they were nevertheless interesting. The report found that 96 percent of organizations used video as part of their training and development strategy. However, only 40 percent of organizations listed it as a key part of their strategy in 2009. This represents a considerable uptake and suggests to me that video's use in the industry has matured. When asked to identify the biggest barrier to making their own videos, just over half of respondents listed time. Reducing the time it takes to craft training videos is important, and, in this book, the techniques I explore can significantly chip away at production time.

The report also found that most of the videos produced by training professionals were used as part of courses, as short tutorials, and as supplements to classroom learning. They were made available through learning management systems and file sharing. Additionally, three-quarters of respondents used screen-capture software such as Camtasia and Articulate. More people were using video captions to make their videos accessible. What also interested me was that many people who participated in the survey used the word *video* to denote a file type. In this book, you'll notice when I say *video*, I am talking about a communication modality (not a file type).

Training Videos

Our profession loves buzzwords—microlearning, blended learning, synchronous and asynchronous learning. I could go on. While not all jargon is helpful, there is value in having descriptive terms that let us know we're all talking about the same thing.

In an emerging discipline like using video to provoke workplace learning, it can be challenging because different terms are thrown around—learning video, instructional video, training video, microvideo, screen recording, explainer video, MOOC (massive open online course), educational video, and so on. It's further complicated because some folks create slide decks, add narration, and then call it video. Sure, it's a video file, but is it really video?

None of these terms are perfect, nor clearly defined. So, in this book, I use the term *training videos*, which are instructional videos that are self-planned, self-filmed, and self-edited by trainers, instructional designers, and learning experience professionals. I'm not talking about live videos, like lectures delivered on Zoom or Webex, or videos outsourced to professional production companies. Rather, training videos are videos that learning professionals produce to show in a physical or virtual classroom to support learning and that they embed in e-learning modules or upload to YouTube or learning experience platforms. In this book, I am especially focused on training videos filmed for next-to-no cost using easily accessible equipment like smartphones and affordable editing software. "No cost" doesn't mean amateur or second rate—I am presenting videos that intentionally follow professional media principles in planning and production.

That said, I will not be using the term video to describe simple slide decks with recorded narration and exported as a video file or sequences of still photos set to inspirational music. I'm not disparaging those forms of content, but they do not fall into this book's scope. Training videos show moving action over time and are mostly captured on your phone's video camera, recorded with screen-capture software, or crafted using animation software.

Selling Video to Your Boss

Video production has fast become an important part of the learning professional's skill set. So, selling the idea of investing time in making training videos that support learning to your boss or client isn't as tough as it used to be. The bigger struggle will likely be how many resources are allocated for production. Some people mistakenly think videos can be thrown together quickly because that's what happens on YouTube. (They conveniently forget those videos often lack good production.) Well-produced and intentional training videos generally take three to four hours of production for every final minute. However, the investment pays off with easier-to-understand content and better retention. So, selling to your boss is more about asking for time and resources. What arguments can you offer?

- **Save money.** You can record one video of a SME explaining a complex subject and use it multiple times, rather than asking them to leave their desk repeatedly during the year to be a guest in a training program. You can also avoid costly field trips that involve learners going to a worksite and looking at equipment—the video can bring it to them instead.
- **Make training more relevant.** You can film real life and show it in the classroom, which beats photos and diagrams on slide decks. An up-close video of a mechanic featuring slow-motion replay to emphasize key elements is much more effective than gathering 15 people in a workshop around a piece of gear and hoping their eyes catch the relevant action.
- **Make demonstrations more instructional.** Whether changing a car tire, replacing a toner cartridge, or highlighting body language, it's great to perform demonstrations in a classroom. Video allows you to replay the demo, focus on key aspects, and perform slow-motion replays.
- **Better serve global teams.** If you have teams scattered globally in different time zones, you can make an on-demand video available to whoever needs it, whenever they need it. They don't

need to watch your live webinar at 2 a.m., but they can hit the play button when it suits them.

- **Be more learner centric.** The best training is provided when it's needed, where it's needed, and on the learner's terms. Don't force learners to sit through loads of irrelevant content. Rather, allow them to zero in on only what they need. On-demand videos can be watched when and where the learner wants. Also, short videos are granular and more focused, which ensures learners aren't forced to sit through presentations that are irrelevant or about content they are already familiar with.

The Dynamics of Video

It's not uncommon for instructional designers to sit in a meeting with clients or SMEs and talk for an hour about a video, each leaving with a different expectation of the final product. That's because there are so many dynamics to video that affect how it is experienced by the learner, including the visual format, filming style, where it is accessed, and whether it is recorded or live.

Is Video a Medium or Modality?

It's easy to think that video is a medium. It's what many people think of when they hear the term "multimedia learning," which implies the use of audio, video, text, and graphics. But, for our purposes, video is a modality. Twenty-five years ago, video was mostly accessed via a TV at home or on a big screen at the cinema. Today, it's consumed on phones, tablets, and desktop computers, as well as projected on a screen hanging on a training room wall. Because it was an inseparable part of the TV medium, video was often referred to as a medium itself, especially in journalism and film schools. No matter if the content was a movie or TV newscast, you'd hear people talking about the video medium. But when video burst into the web space, it didn't bring the TV with it—the medium that carried it. At its core, video is simply moving pictures with sound—a modality. Video co-exists on the web and on digital platforms with other communication modalities, such as text, graphics, and standalone audio. While it's tempting to think of the web as the new medium, it's actually a network that connects us to different modalities, like the airwaves that connect us to TV or radio. The real medium is the device you use to watch videos, such as your phone or laptop (Halls 2016b). So, as I talk about modalities and mediums in this book, *medium* refers to the physical device hosting content (such as a radio, TV, or tablet) and *modality* describes the form of content the medium is hosting (such as audio, video, text, or graphics).

Visual Formats

Because there is no universal system to categorize the visual formats you see in video, I'll reference different formats in this book using these terms:

- **Optical-sequence video** involves capturing multiple action shots using a video camera and editing them into a sequence. For example, shots from different positions and angles can be used to convey a message on TV in news packages, documentaries, and drama series. The action is optically captured through a video camera lens, and the video intentionally conveys a message with multiple shots in a sequence, unlike seeing someone talking about the action.
- **Talking-head video** refers to someone talking to the camera, such as in a filmed monologue. In training, this could be a teacher talking for 10 minutes. It may include cutting between the talking head and text graphics. It is arguably the least effective video format because it's boring and people easily forget the information. However, it's often used in training because it's cheap and easy to produce.
- **Screen-capture video** is when a computer or mobile device's screen is recorded while someone is performing a function; it's then edited into a sequence. It's common in training, especially for software training videos. It's typically produced using tools such as Camtasia or Articulate.
- **Animated-sequence video** is similar to optical-sequence video except the footage is not captured by a camera; instead, it's

drawn or illustrated, as in traditional cartoons like *Looney Tunes*. The moving images can be drawn frame by frame but are more commonly created using graphics and animation software, like Vyond, Powtoon, or Animaker.

- **Animated graphics** refer to schematic drawings. For example, an animated graphic could show how a nuclear reactor works. Often, they can be part of an optical-sequence or talking-head video, although they can also be standalone with interactive features that users click to reveal certain elements or review experiential learning sequences.
- **360-degree video** means the user can interactively move the camera to see all around it. This format can be effective in e-learning, but it's not a focus of this book because I'm looking at how to craft content that people watch, rather than interact with.
- **Virtual reality** involves users wearing goggles to get a 3D sense of reality. This powerful format is used in simulations such as flight simulators. However, it too is beyond the scope of this book and is expensive to produce.

The number of visual formats available to learning professionals is exciting, but it's unrealistic to explore them in any real depth in a book like this—each one has enough important dynamics to warrant its own book. That's why my focus is on making optical-sequence videos. However, I will take detours from time to time to consider the key dynamics and best practices of talking-head videos, screen-capture videos, and animated videos because they follow the same visual engagement principles as optical-sequence videos.

Video Styles

Videographers often adopt a specific style when filming and editing content. For example, a documentary might follow a fly-on-the-wall filming style so viewers can see events unfold naturally, like in National Geographic's *Naked and Afraid*. BBC documentaries hosted by David Attenborough, such as Planet Earth, follow an expository approach in which a narrator presents information showing carefully constructed sequences. Documentaries may also follow a news style in which a presenter talks from behind a desk or a reporter speaks to the camera from a specific location. The run-and-gun technique involves the videographer responding spontaneously to events and filming in the moment, which often features shaky camera work and gives the footage a gritty realism. Contrast this style with formal documentaries that are carefully choreographed, and the filming technique is much more subtle.

Live Versus Prerecorded

Initially, training videos were prerecorded and available either as part of a sequence of online learning experiences or on demand. They were embedded into e-learning modules, used as part of virtual and physical training sessions, and made available on demand through a content library. However, video platforms now allow video to be streamed live and thisbecame a common practice during the COVID-19 pandemic with remote work. Live video is a regular feature of social media platforms like LinkedIn, YouTube, and Facebook. It is also a key aspect of virtual learning events that involve an instructor appearing on screen while showing a slide deck or video clips. Although I am not specifically discussing live video in this book, many of the video principles are the same.

Where Video Is Hosted and Accessed

The viewing experience will be different depending on where videos are hosted and viewed. Hosting options include YouTube, Facebook, Instagram, TikTok, and other social media sites, as well as in online courses hosted by platforms like Udemy or Teachable. In the corporate world, videos will likely be embedded in courses hosted on learning management systems or learning experience platforms. The experience the platform creates for viewing the video (such as where it locates buttons, like play, pause, fast forward, and rewind) and visual distractions that exist on the screen (like ads or thumbnails of related videos) will affect how the viewer takes in the information from your video.

Where viewers watch the video also affects how they take in the content. Professional video used to be viewed either on TV or in the cinema, which both offer very different experiences. The cinema is immersive and a viewer can pivot their head from left to right to watch a horse gallop across the screen. Dimmed lights limit distractions, and the Dolby Digital sound wraps around the audience. TV, on the other hand, offers a more distracted experience. It's likely on the other side of a well-lit room and enjoyed while families prepare dinner or kids do homework. To create engaging and memorable content for these contexts requires different production styles and techniques. Today, you also need to consider what works for newer devices such as computer screens, tablets, and mobile phones.

What Does All This Mean?

Video immediately sounds like a smart idea for many learning situations, so many people assume that anyone can produce video today. For this reason, more than 96 percent of organizations have incorporated video as an important part of their learning and talent strategy (Halls 2021). But not everyone can produce good video. It takes intentionality and well-developed skills requiring practitioners to follow practices and workflows that ensure high quality and efficiency. Not all video is created equally because you can adopt multiple visual formats and editorial styles. And the way a video is experienced can differ depending on what platform people view it on. They key for learning professionals is to be intentional and focused because that's what leads to consistently good video.

How to Plan for the Future of Video

WITH MATT PIERCE

Key takeaways:
- The last 10 years have made video easy for anyone to make.
- AI will give us incredible editing tools, but we need to keep the human connection.
- When using new technology, ask if it will support learning or if it's just a trend.

You might call Matt Pierce a fixture in the training video space. He's been speaking at conferences and hosting podcasts on training videos for as long as I can remember. In a field that sees thought leaders come and go every few years, he's been a steady presence.

So, what does he think are the key developments? Where does he think we're headed?

We've Had a Lot of Change

"I think one of the biggest developments has been just the ability to create video," Matt says. "Ten years ago, you needed to be specialized with the right gear to create video. Now, we literally carry a powerful camera wherever we go.

"The ability to create on the fly is huge," he reflects, "along with the ability to distribute video. Yes, we had YouTube and other hosting sites 10 years ago, but now everyone has accounts and can upload to YouTube, TikTok, Instagram, Facebook, and Twitter."

Another gamechanger has been file size and picture quality. "Ten years ago, video file sizes had to be very small, around four to 10 megabytes. Now, I routinely upload video files of 200 or 300 megabytes.

"Style has changed too. We used to make horizontal video, but now vertical video is accessible to platforms that are actually prioritizing it."

What's Next?

"The generation portion of video creation will be immensely expedited. AI tools that allow you to change the dynamic and the modality of how you edit are the future. We'll see tools that let us edit video like a document. Now, the challenge with AI is that we're giving up autonomy, right? I love the idea of AI helping out, but I don't want to lose the human connection."

Matt sees many of the developments leaning toward making video production easier, whether you're producing things like motion graphics or making editorial decisions.

"We're seeing a lot of automation to help make video decisions faster and easier," he says. "I think some of this will happen through templating systems."

Key Questions for the Future

Having been actively involved in the video space for the past decade, what questions does Matt think we need to ask to stay ahead of the game as the use of video in training continues to develop at an exciting pace?

"The key questions are not necessarily about video technology because that's going to evolve rapidly," he says. "It's a lot more about learning modalities. When thinking of technology, we need to ask, does this tool better help my audience understand or perform? And, if the answer is yes, then this is a good idea." The question relates to results too. "Am I getting better quality and better results with this technology? If not, ask, should I be using it?"

He adds that we "need to think about connection and keeping it real. How does the technology ensure we keep our humanity?"

While he doesn't specifically ask if we are doing video for the sake of video, he said he often reflects on animated whiteboard videos, which raises a question. "This may be a personal bias of mine. Seeing white-board animation was great the first or second time I saw it; after that, every other one looked the same." Referring to Maslow's famous hammer and nail quote, he suggested that these videos were someone's hammer, and every learning need was a nail.

"Be thoughtful when using video content," Matt advises. "Is it right for the audience? Is it going to improve the work and outcomes? Or, is it something that's just a trend or a style? You can always jump into the trend, but know it's a trend so you can be willing to jump out too."

Matt Pierce is the host of The Visual Lounge podcast by TechSmith; connect with Matt at linkedin.com/in/matthewrpierce.

Chapter 2
The Learning Formula

In this chapter, you'll learn about:
- How training videos can help people learn
- Structuring video content by drawing on people's existing experiences
- The importance of repetition to enable retrieval and improve retention
- Using training videos as a tool in the learning process

A popular conversation among trainers making videos is whether to aim for high or low production values. *High production* means TV quality with fancy graphics and effects like using a green screen. *Low production* videos may be only slightly more polished than Uncle Seth's wobbly home videos from last summer's family reunion. It's a passionate discussion because some trainers really want their videos to be broadcast quality. Perhaps they're budding TV journalists or harbor secret dreams of working in Hollywood. On the other hand, some folks turn their nose up at TV quality videos—labeling them contrived and inauthentic. Maybe they want to spend a little less time producing video and don't mind compromising quality for short cuts.

It's not a debate I want to dig into, but I think the answer lies somewhere in between the two extremes. Slick TV values aren't better or worse than amateur style productions, and the purpose of training videos is neither to look slick nor gritty—it's to help people learn how to do stuff, like change a car tire, learn some open body language, or install an app on their smartphone. So, adopt whatever production value most helps the viewer learn the task. If gritty and authentic is more effective at helping people learn, fantastic. But if it's so unstructured that learning is more difficult, then a more formulaic approach, such as what you see on TV, could make more sense.

However, the professional video production field has much to offer. News production techniques teach you about fast production because newsrooms must turn multiple stories around fast every day. Hollywood can teach you powerful narrative methods and ways to keep viewers' eyes on the screen. And reality TV shows or high-end documentaries offer valuable tips on crafting content to be easy to understand quickly. That said, you shouldn't directly replicate what they do because those genres exist for different purposes.

So, it makes sense to think about learning and how it happens before we go into video. For thousands of years, smart people have postulated what learning is and how it happens, and many contradict one another. Some formed opinions based on observation, others common sense, others conjecture, and others research. Without wading too much into various theories and controversies, I will take a stab at describing (not defining) *learning* by drawing on some of the key influencers in the field of adult education. Then, I'll discuss how learning happens so I can outline the role that training videos play in the learning process.

What Is Learning?

When defining learning in corporate training, folks often turn to the adult learning principles promoted by Malcolm Knowles from the late 1960s to the 1980s. He defined *learning* as the process of gaining knowledge or expertise (Knowles, Holton, and Swanson 2005). Robert Gagne (1965), another key influencer, noted that capabilities derived from learning are retained and are not just something developed through growth. Interesting thoughts spring from these ideas. First, learning is a process. Second, it's intentional. I'm not talking about accidental learning here—that's something different. Third, learning is about retention so learners can perform a task after learning it.

Knowles's definition refers to *knowledge* or *expertise*, but Gagne uses the word *capability*. Assembling multiple definitions is a challenge because of the different nuances and values of each one. I prefer the word *skills*, which is more prevalent in corporate training today. So, channeling Bloom's taxonomy of learning, which suggests learning falls into one of three domains, I'll stick with the idea that learning leads to skills that could be intellectual (cognitive), physical (psychomotor), or mindset (affective; Bloom et al. 1956).

For this book, I suggest that *learning* is the intentional process of building skills. This is something the learner must do—not a trainer, professor, or teacher, but the learner. Learning doesn't happen in a presentation, session plan, or slide deck. It doesn't happen at the front of a classroom or on a webcam. It happens in the learner's brain. It's also a physiological activity, proven by countless brain scan studies that show neurochemical transmitters firing across the brain's synapses as people think. This fact has important implications for training videos, which can't ensure learning because the learner ensures learning. This seemingly straightforward idea is important for making sense of how you can use video to move performance.

So, how does learning happen? Knowing this will help you figure out the role of video in learning. The brain isn't a magic box where stuff goes in raw and comes out baked as skills (which is an assumption many trainers make and in fact describes the behaviorism school of thought).

With a thirst for understanding what happens in the brain, the cognitive psychology field took off in the 1950s and 1960s when scientists started to investigate where the brain focuses its attention and how it makes decisions. The "cognitive revolution" was also fueled by the development of mathematical modeling and led to important ideas of how the brain processes new information, remembers it, and applies it (Malmberg, Raaijmakers, and Shiffrin 2019). I don't believe anyone can confidently say they know everything about learning, and I don't think cognitive research offers the last word. But cognitive science is one of the best places to start.

How Learning Happens

There are many ways to understand the learning process. I break it into three steps called the learning formula (Halls 2019):

$$Understanding + Memory + Application = Learning$$

In the spirit of British statistician George Box, who said, "All models are wrong, but some are useful," I'm quick to say this formula is imperfect (although that doesn't stop it from making sense of what someone needs to do to learn). When you break learning into these three stages, you can be more intentional and plan learning experiences that have clarity around things you can't do. Let's explore each step of this model.

1. Build Understanding

The first step of learning a skill is to understand it—comprehend how to perform that skill and grasp its core concepts. Understanding is all about memory and how the brain processes memories. Human beings make sense of the world through their memories. For example, if you tell me about a trip you took on the Tube during a vacation in London, I will use my memories of traveling to work on the Tube to make sense of your comments. I'll also enrich my understanding of your experience by drawing on my emotions related to traveling on the Tube. If you describe an incident that took place in a science class, I'll dig into memories of my time in school and think about your experience as if it happened in the same science lab I sat in. Of course, if I had not lived in London, or in fact had never heard of the Tube, I might think you were referring to plumbing, not an underground train system. I need some initial knowledge to make sense of what you're talking about.

At a high level, helping learners build understanding is simple. Provide a stimulus for them to dig into their long-term memory for a memory they can use to sift through the new information you are presenting. For example, if I'm in the classroom teaching organizational change management, I might first ask if you have ever experienced major change—perhaps moving to a new house or getting married. Then, I might ask how you felt during the change. By drawing on this memory, you can gain a practical understanding to make sense of the emotional impact organizational change can have on workers. It's no different in video, except you're using moving pictures (something I'll discuss later), along with sound and graphic effects, music, and commentary to help people connect to an appropriate memory. For example, if I see an image of a school bus, it triggers a memory of school that I can use to understand the message you're presenting. If I see an image of lots of cars parked together, I'll think it's a parking lot. If that image also includes a sign in that says, "Departures This Way," I'll pull from my memories in airports to realize that it's an airport parking lot. And it's not just visual cues. Music will do the same thing. Have you ever noticed how you recall certain emotions when you hear a song that was popular in your final year of high school?

As I discussed earlier, the learner must do the work of constructing an understanding. You can't do it for them. You can provide the information, but they must supply the memory they will use to think about it. I like to think of building understanding as a process that connects existing memories with new information (which is also a memory). Your role as a trainer is to help learners make these connections and encourage them to process it (think about it), which leads to comprehension. You should help them find the most appropriate memory, but that requires you to know your audience well. I'll discuss this more when I consider the familiarity principle in chapter 4.

So far, I've described memories in the brain, but what exactly are they? There are many theories; some refer to memories as *associations*, others as *patterns*, and others as *mental models* or *representations*. Cambridge psychologist Frederick Bartlett (1932) offers the schema theory concept. *Schemas* are internal mental representations of concepts, facts, and experiences. Educational psychologist David Rumelhart (1980) describes them as the building blocks of comprehension. The better organized the model, the more effective it is for people functioning in their lives, just as people organize their desks so they can find the items they need. Our brains constantly seek order to manage our memories by arranging information into structures. Schema is closely associated with the term *schematic diagrams*, and it may help to think of schema as a diagram you follow to perform a task. Another metaphor is how computer software turns data into something meaningful. People have schemas for everything in life, from how to take the trash out, to how to fry an egg, to whether your children are naughty or well behaved, and to which political party has the right take on the world. (The correct grammar when referring to the plural of schemas, is *schemata*. However, using the word *schemas* as the plural form has gained traction because it seems more accessible to folks. It is becoming adopted by popular usage, so I'm adopting that spelling in this book.)

All trainers see their roles in different ways. For me, learning professionals are in the business of helping learners build schemas. According to Rumelhart and Norman (1978), there are three modes of learning, or ways to build schemas:

- **Accretion.** Add new information to an existing schema. For example, every state in the US has a capital city. So, with a schema to represent this, you just need to learn the capital cities, which can be done by adding the name of each capital and associating it with the correct state.
- **Restructuring.** Start with nothing and construct the schema from scratch. Restructuring occurs when you learn brand-new concepts that don't fit into an existing schema. I'm not much of a sport person—in fact, I'm not one at all—so when I go to a baseball game with my wife (who has to explain what's happening because I'm more interested in the nachos), I have to build a brand-new structure to organize the game in my mind.
- **Tuning.** Change an existing schema into a new one to make sense of new information or an entirely new topic. If you want

to teach me how to drive a bus, you might sit in the driver's seat and ask, "Have you ever driven a car?" I have. "What instruments did you use?" I used the steering wheel, gear stick, gas pedal, clutch, and break. So, you tell me that "It's the same for a bus." I'm using my schema for driving a car to understand how to drive a bus. But it's not the right schema, so you have to help me either build a new one or modify this one. For example, "Jonathan, how many gears have you had in your cars?" Five. So, you then tell me, "With a bus, you will have nine gears." You might then help me understand that lower gears are appropriate for certain conditions like driving in snow.

Accretion and tuning are the easiest ways to build schemas. Restructuring is difficult. Most of the time a person connects existing knowledge, which their brain organizes as schemas, to new information. Then, their brain either adds to an existing schema or uses it as a template to build a new one. Clapp and Devine (2023) describe existing knowledge as a building block that you add new knowledge to, which, when connected to concepts you already know, makes learning quicker and easier. The question to remember for training videos is how to use this modality to build schemas.

2. Build Memory

There's no reason to understand a concept or the series of steps needed to complete a task if you can't remember them when it's time to use them. That is what the second step of the learning formula is all about: building memory, which involves saving the learning (a new schema) into the long-term memory (LTM) so it can be recalled when needed. It's great to understand how to change a car tire while parked in my driveway, but if I can't remember how to do it when stranded on the side of the road, I'm in a pickle. Again, this is something that the learner must do, and it involves a retrieval process.

When you research memory, you'll find many references to LTM, short-term memory (STM), and working memory (WM). These relate to a model proposed in 1968 by Atkinson and Shiffrin, who suggest that the brain processes information between sensory input (the sensory register), STM, and LTM. The model has evolved since then; for example, most learning professionals use WM rather than STM based on subsequent research by Baddeley and Fitch (1974), but the general model underpins much of today's research and discussion of memory.

LTM is like a computer's hard drive. It's where schemas are saved. WM is like a computer's RAM, where new information connects to existing schemas that are saved in the LTM to enable understanding (step one in the learning formula). WM passes the new information through the schema to make sense of it as it creates a new schema for the new information. The sensory register is like a gatekeeper that prohibits unnecessary information from entering the WM, which is important because the WM has a very limited capacity. Most of the information that gets past the sensory register into WM is forgotten because the brain seems wired to forget stuff. This was famously demonstrated in 1885 by German psychologist Herman Ebbinghaus—his Forgetting Curve model shows that within an hour of a presentation, almost 60 percent of the information was forgotten. Clapp and Devine (2023) describe this process of forgetting or discarding information as a matter of efficiency for the brain to optimize performance.

To remember something, you must take deliberate action to encode it in the LTM. This action, known as *retrieval,* is a key part of memory consolidation and involves retrieving the memory (or schema) into the WM. Studies in both cognitive science and neuroscience show that this process creates pathways to a memory. Forms of retrieval are also referred to by some researchers as *practice* and *rehearsal.* The more often you retrieve a memory, the stronger the connection to that memory becomes. In everyday language, retrieval translates to practicing something, talking about it, and reflecting on it. Therefore, the most valuable part of an L&D experience is most likely when participants practice or discuss a skill rather than when a trainer gives a presentation. However, some forms of retrieval are more effective than others. One form called *blocked practice* involves reciting or performing something repeatedly. It can make memory acquisition easier, but it impairs long-term retention. High contextual interference—which interrupts this process by practicing multiple skills in succession—leads to better long-term retention (Brady 1998). Types of practice that cause interference and lead to better memory include spaced practice and interleaving (Martina, Vincent, and Rummel 2013).

The process of retrieving memories from the LTM strengthens recall, effectively making something easier to remember.

OK, I know I've gone into geek territory here, so let's regroup and think about what this means for video. Building understanding is about connecting new information with existing knowledge and skills, which are saved in the LTM as schemas. Because our brains are wired to forget new knowledge, as a matter of efficiency, the learner must actively work to encode it into the LTM through retrieval or practice. As a trainer, you design activities in your classes that push learners into retrieving these new memories, knowing that the more they do, the stronger the memories will be. Activities could be discussing new concepts, practicing new skills, doing observations and critiques, and journaling. This is precisely where the magic of memory encoding happens.

But video can't do any of this. It can't force the learner into practice. It can't ensure that the retrieval process or cognitive engagement happens. It is merely a tool the learner might use to build their understanding.

So, hold that thought for a few moments. I suggested earlier that, in some ways, WM is like your computer's RAM. It connects new information to existing memories in your LTM, like a computer retrieves a software program from the hard drive, and then into the WM to make sense of data. But there's a significant difference between WM and RAM. As technology advances, the capacity of computer RAM continually increases to handle more complex computations. Five years ago, my computers had 4 gigabytes of RAM. Today, it's exponentially higher. But the human brain cannot expand, and WM has a notoriously low capacity. While different studies suggest different capacities, all of them rate

WM capacity as low. One study suggests that WM can only hold three to five chunks of information at one time (Cowan 2010). This means that it can be easily overloaded if you try to give it too much information. I'll explore the implications of this later.

3. Apply Learning

The goal of L&D extends beyond understanding and remembering new skills. Training is about allowing workers to apply their skills on the job, which is the third component of the learning formula. This final application stage is not a result, but rather a continuum that stretches from novice level performance to mastery. It requires practice and the addition of expert feedback to guide practice through increasingly complex levels of performance, which is something else that video cannot do. Applying and developing skills starts in a classroom but mostly happens on the job. You need practice with feedback to strengthen the connections to schemas and hone performance.

Video has much less of a role in the application stage because this stage is fueled by practice and feedback. However, you can influence the application stage by expanding how you see training videos and considering the learning as something that extends well beyond physical video. You could create job aids like checklists or cheat sheets for learners to carry with them when practicing a task. Every time you create a training video, you could consider providing a PDF with instructions or an infographic that summarizes key steps. You could also share additional resources like job aids for managers to provide effective feedback.

What Does All This Mean?

Adopting video as a key learning tool means facing some challenges. As I've discussed, learning is something that happens in the learner's brain. They will construct their skills by connecting new content with schemas in their LTM. That's where the learning takes place. But unlike in a classroom—where a trainer can see that participants have glazed eyes and quickly adjust delivery pace, switch out content to better meet their needs, or get them moving around the room to wake them up—video is fixed. Video can't adapt or force anyone to be engaged, even if the content is interesting. So, you need to think about ways to spur engagement. While this is outside this book's scope, the impact of video will be greatly enhanced if it is dovetailed into the broader education strategy. For example, as you create your video, also plan job aids for learners to support their memory and checklists and tip sheets for experts who are giving feedback in the application stage. Think about incorporating quizzes and interactive experiences like games that can push learners to engage in the content. For example, produce videos alongside a quick quiz or game that forces learners to retrieve key knowledge. Or organize a cohort in which people discuss or journal key information. The purpose of video is to spur cognitive processing.

Chapter 3
Supporting Learning Through Video

In this chapter, you'll learn about:
- Mayers' multimedia theory
- The research around video in L&D
- Key principles, including signaling, segmenting, and weeding

Chapter 2 probably wasn't a heavy lift—most learning professionals have a good understanding of how learning happens. The learning formula is one of many ways to make sense of the steps learners take to build skills. In this chapter, I cover research related to training videos and share my thoughts on why we need more specific research. I suspect that those with a more practical mindset may be tempted to skip it. That's fine—just don't miss chapter 4, which is where I put it all into practice. If you're interested in how to best support learning using video, read on.

When I wrote *Rapid Video Development for Trainers* in 2012, there were very few studies that were immediately relevant to what makes good video content in the L&D space, such as content viewed on a corporate LMS or as a performance support tool. For example, I couldn't find acceptable evidence-based answers to the questions "How do you structure a video to ensure learning?" or "How do you ensure retention?" So, I drew on what was considered good practice in TV production, skewed no doubt from what I learned during my time at the BBC, and mashed it with key cognitive learning principles. The studies that existed then were usually in a different context from L&D. And few got into elements of fully packaged video—such as how to frame shots and use music, when to feature voiceovers, and what to do with other visual elements, like text graphics, to better provoke comprehension.

Many instructional designers instinctively look to Richard E. Mayer's (2020) multimedia principles when thinking through video production because it's full of important concepts. But they are not video-specific and they apply to all modalities. Mayer is probably the most prolific researcher in the field and has provided enormous insight through his research into what makes good multimedia—his principles of multimedia instructional design are based on more than 200 experimental studies grounded in cognitive psychology.

I know other folks who were working with training videos, some of whom I worked with in TV. They weren't armed with research but instead followed well-honed production instincts forged over years of making educational content. Interestingly, many of the good TV production techniques they followed have been shown by education studies to provoke learning, such as keeping videos short, cutting between slides and head shots, writing scripts that are conversational rather than formal, and removing irrelevant content elements. This chapter will draw on Mayer and other researchers to consider how their theories can be applied to L&D while also highlighting the need for more research.

Mayer's Multimedia Theory

Richard Mayer's cognitive theory of multimedia learning sets out principles for creating digital content that supports learning. His principles parallel what has been considered good practice in TV for decades, although those evolved from practice rather than research. Mayer's (2020) multimedia principles fall into three categories:

- **Remove unnecessary information** in multimedia messages to reduce what he calls "extraneous processing."

- **Manage the learning load** so it does not overwhelm the learner but, instead, allows space for deeper reflection. He calls this "managing essential processing."
- **Personalize the learning experience** to foster generative processing to deepen the learning.

While his principles aren't all directly relevant to the kind of videos I am talking about in this book, most are instructive. For example, the personalization principle suggests that people learn best when a voice-over or narration element in a training video is delivered in an informal, conversational tone (Schrader, Reichelt, and Zander 2018). Therefore, a narrator should say, "You will find," as opposed to, "Viewers will find." Again, it's interesting how research parallels practice in broadcasting. I've taught broadcast writing on and off since the late 1980s, and a key principle for broadcast scripts is to write in a conversational tone. You see this in key journalism texts, from Robert L. Hilliard's *Writing for Television, Radio, and New Media* to BBC news veteran Vin Ray's *The Television News Handbook*. As Ray (2003) puts it, "Write the way you talk in polite conversation . . . as if telling a friend or just one viewer. When you try telling the same story to just one person your language becomes more conversational, and your language becomes simpler and more direct."

Closely related is Mayer's voice principle theory, which asserts that people learn better from a human voice as opposed to a computer-generated one and that learning is boosted if the voice has an enthusiastic expression as opposed to slow, carefully read narration in a calm, emotionless voice (Liew et al. 2020). Again, this principle echoes a traditional media practice that involves highly trained actors reading voice-overs and bringing pace, pitch, and expression to their delivery. Traditional media folks don't usually seek research into why these things work other than studying content that rates well and gets awards. So, they adopt practices handed down from experience.

Mayer's multimedia principles support many of the techniques in this book that I've drawn from traditional broadcasting. His is not the only research relevant to instructional videos, but it's probably the most useful.

How Much Can You Rely on Research?

A commonly quoted study from Philip J. Guo, Juho Kim, and Rob Rubin (2014) shares some practical tips specifically for making instructional video more effective. They found that among other things:

- **Shorter videos are more engaging.** They suggest videos should be less than six minutes long.
- **Showing slides with a faceless narrator is not as effective** as cutting between a slide and a presenter.
- **Videos with instructors who speak fast with enthusiastic expression are more engaging** than those with an instructor who tries to sound formal and slows their delivery to enunciate every word.

What draws many people to this study is its sample size. The researchers drew on the responses from 6.9 million video viewing sessions, which, frankly, is stratospheric. It's hard to argue against any of their suggestions, and why would you? These tips also parallel common TV practices that have been used for decades. If you sit a 20-year TV veteran down over a pint of beer, they'll tell you the same things, having never read an ounce of research. I'm not trying to downplay the value of research. Rather, I'm celebrating the congruity between research and what's learned in practice.

However, you must read more than just the summaries because some research may not be as relevant as you think. For example, that 2014 study was on video engagement in massive open online courses (MOOCs), "which is a university course that is openly available to unlimited numbers of participants, free of charge" (Porter 2015). As far as pedagogy is concerned, MOOCs have more in common with distance and academic education than workplace L&D. It's a different context with different dynamics. For example, MOOCs may include hundreds or even thousands of participants watching synchronously, have no entry requirements, and be delivered online with no contiguous or face-to-face contact. Like a traditional university course, they have a prescribed curriculum and generally involve some form of assessment

(Porter 2015). We just don't do this sort of thing in L&D—our content is much less learner directed and focused on practical activities like being a good leader or using an Excel spreadsheet. University education is topic focused; for example, the first MOOC explored the education theory of connectivism. Corporate training videos are used more often in the following contexts (Halls 2021):

- As part of a course
- As a short tutorial
- To supplement classroom training
- As performance support

A further complication in the research is that there are so many video formats. There are optical-sequence videos (which I focus on in this book), screen-capture videos, talking-head videos, live recordings of professors presenting in a lab, animations, and even PowerPoint slides with narration. These variances present challenges for researchers, which is why you must generalize your findings. Add to that challenge the question of who should be surveyed. For example, are university students' outlooks, interests, motivations, and experiences different from busy staffers in corporate environments, where video is often produced for performance support or to supplement classroom training?

Researchers often make conclusions based on peoples' different assumptions about what a word means. In chapter 1, I defined *training videos* because so many people used that phrase to describe different things, drawing conclusions they then applied to things that weren't the same. Let's say I conduct a study to see how many people like eggs. I hire a good chef to cook the most incredibly creamy, buttery, herb-infused, and yummy serving of scrambled eggs and have 500 people try them. Isn't the best way to figure out if someone likes eggs to have them taste eggs? Assuming my survey goes well, maybe 60 percent check the box that indicates they didn't like them. That could lead me to conclude that most people don't like eggs. After all, I checked whether they liked eggs. But is that a fair assessment of whether people like eggs? If I served poached, fried, or boiled eggs, I might get an entirely different response. To assess whether people like eggs by simply serving one form is misleading, and not just because of how the eggs were cooked, but also the very style of scrambled eggs. What if the chef served scrambled eggs that weren't buttery or creamy? Some folks might prefer that over the creamy ones, which would lead to a different result.

You may think I'm belaboring a point about research—of course, it's open to different conclusions. My point is that one of the biggest limitations of research into video is the different types of video (screen captures, talking heads, animation, and PowerPoint narrations, among others) and you can't apply one result to all forms. If research says people lose interest in and don't like to watch long videos, then you can apply that conclusion to talking-head videos but not necessarily to optical-sequence videos, which are more highly crafted and have more action and shot changes. People may watch longer optical-sequence videos, and while the research doesn't yet confirm this, I'd suggest they would. There's also another interesting dynamic that might affect results—the people who are studied. A lot of psychology research is conducted on university students. To measure the effectiveness of training videos, would it be better to do so with people using them in the workplace under the pressure of their work, rather than younger folks at university?

I'm not saying research is unhelpful. Rather, we have a long way to go before understanding in detail what makes a good training video. It's early days because so many dynamics and assumptions are at play and words are being defined and used differently across the spectrum. We need to balance video research with what we can learn from the world of TV and other media production practices and use that to innovate new ways of crafting content.

Signaling, Segmenting, and Weeding

So, while you can learn broad principles from Guo, Kim, and Rubin as well as from other studies, you should be cautious when following studies too closely without knowing more specifics—like what type of video they're talking about and how it is structured and framed. I'm more inclined to draw general conventions than black-and-white rules that say videos need to include X to achieve Y.

In the spirit of a more generalized perspective, I'd like to discuss some empirical studies that highlight three principles for making engaging video content that manages cognitive load. These add to the Guo, Kim, and Rubin's important study and draw from Mayer's principles. They also fit nicely into the general practice that broadcasters have developed over the years.

A study from India found that when video was produced following Mayer's principles, student performance can be demonstrably better (Dash, Kamath, Rao, Prakash, and Mishra 2016). To manage cognitive load, it's important to employ three techniques:

- **Signaling** occurs when you use text or graphics to highlight part of the screen that has key information. For example, in a text graphic, you may have three bullets and highlight one in a different color to direct the viewer's attention. In a screen-capture video, you might zoom in or cut to a close-up of a region on the screen, such as drop-down menu.
- **Segmenting** is breaking longer content into shorter chunks. You'll remember Guo, Kim, and Rubin found videos worked best when they were shorter than six minutes. Breaking a 20-minute video into four, five-minute videos gives learners a chance to stop and process key content. Segmenting could be used as part of an asynchronous unit of online learning for quizzes or activities that provoke learning.
- **Weeding** refers to pulling out unnecessary information. This could include complex backgrounds or irrelevant props left in frame. The less there is to process, the lower the cognitive load, which supports learning because of WM's limited load capability.

Together, these three techniques illuminate abstract or hard-to-visualize phenomena for the learner.

Cognitive Load Theory

Oliver Lovell (2020) describes cognitive load as anything that takes up the WM capacity, the bottleneck of thinking. There are two types of cognitive load. *Extraneous load* is the effort learners make to decode information and make sense of it, which is influenced by how information is taught or presented. *Intrinsic load* is the complexity of the learning topic itself. Cognitive load theory was developed by John Sweller at the University of New South Wales, and it aims to decrease extraneous load while optimizing intrinsic load, which leads to better learning outcomes. You want to produce videos with the lowest cognitive load possible using the best practices outlined in this book.

In another study, a group of researchers at Oklahoma State University decided to test the signaling, segmenting, and weeding principles with a video about insects produced by the BBC in 1994 (Ibrahim et al. 2012). This documentary is an optical-sequence video, so it's closer to what I'm talking about in this book. The researchers took the 32-minute documentary and broke it into five conceptual segments that ran for about six minutes each (segmenting). They also added a summary screen at the end of each section and signals for main concepts (signaling). And with the help of a course instructor, they removed material from the videos that was not relevant to the main points (weeding). The study showed that these actions reduced perceived learning difficulty and cognitive load for the viewer. On the other hand, the study also found that retention was low, proving that even video that reduces cognitive load doesn't necessarily ensure learners will remember the content because memory formation is an important part of learning. I can't help but wonder if this is simply because video can't force the learner to engage with content.

As we explore video production techniques throughout this book, you'll find that traditional practices support segmenting, signaling, and weeding. You will be applying what you know from the cognitive field to create video content that provokes learning.

What Does All This Mean?

It's not my intention to make things more complicated than they need to be. I just want to be careful about blindly following research that offers pithy advice with lists of dos and don'ts as if they were the last word on the matter because there is still so much to learn. I also don't want to reject research either simply because it can't yet reveal everything; we need more specific studies pertaining to video.

So, in this book, the tips I share are in tension with:

- **My professional practice.** What I have been taught in professional media, I have in turn taught around the globe as a professional media trainer in media organizations. Some media practices may not be research-based, but that doesn't mean they are ineffective. They just haven't been interrogated yet.

- **Theory.** Understanding how the brain works, how people learn, and principles for supporting learning with theories that are accepted as academically rigorous is important. I balance what we can learn from thought leaders like Mayer, Atkinson, Shiffrin, Rumelhart, Sweller, and others.

- **Studies.** Research studies from Guo, Kim, and Rubin or Ibrahim, Antonenko, Greenwood, and Wheeler, among others, may be focused on a different type of pedagogy from L&D, but still offer insights you can learn from. The studies are based on theories, such as Mayer's, and they show theory in action.

Of course, I've only just scratched the surface, but you can draw several helpful ideas for making training videos that provoke learning. In the next chapter, I consider some key practices that build on these three areas of interest.

How to Find the Value of Your Videos

WITH NICOLE PAPAIOANNOU LUGARA

Key takeaways:
- Video is a great tool to speed up collaboration, especially in distributed teams.
- Engaging video content should be authentic.
- It's important to be clear about the video's purpose.

Nicole Papaioannou Lugara is all about the personal connection in learning, especially with distributed teams. The more authentic the connection, the better the collaboration. Video is a key tool she uses in her work with clients as the founder and CEO of Your Instructional Designer, based in New Jersey.

She says, "Many of us are working in distributed teams, whether remote or hybrid, or even in frontline work. Workers are stuck on their shift all day, and unless you want to close down the shop, they can't all do training at the same time. Video makes it possible to learn asynchronously. If it's done right, you can feel like you're there with someone, or you can get the information as if you're sitting in the classroom. So, I think it's a wonderful thing.

"Video can be used to create content that's easier to access than just written documentation; for example, to scale up job shadowing. Not everyone can go on-site with an engineer, but you can strap a GoPro on their head while they do their processes and talk it through. Now, you've scaled shadowing so everyone can go on a ride with your senior engineer. It's a very powerful tool for training."

Nicole also notes how "video can provide opportunities for social learning in asynchronous environments by allowing people to listen to others' stories and wisdom or observe them in action." However, "If you think about adult learning, adults want agency over their learning. When video on demand is an option, it allows for learning in the flow of work and for adults to take control over their learning—whether that's the content they consume or the pacing at which they consume it."

What's the Value of Video?

Nicole keeps coming back to the word *authentic* when thinking about video's real value in learning. It's so easy to make these days with accessible tools and a smartphone. "Video is authentic, especially as we move into the age of AI," she says, referring to newer technologies that can generate content.

"It's hard for AI to mimic the crazy things I'm doing with my hands and the sentences I say aloud that are not in perfect grammar. It all helps people feel like they have a connection with a real human." But, she's not against AI. "I want AI to be the tool that helps us do things to get rid of the stuff we don't want to do so we can spend more time coming together and connecting."

Workflow

Does Nicole think a workflow is necessary? She says, "There's a time for a stream of consciousness approach, but, generally, I think you should sit down for a few minutes and ask, what's the purpose? What is the thing I want my learner to take away from this small moment in time?

"Then, think about the journey. Where is the learner now and where does the learner need to be? What are the check-ins and checkpoints? Whether you have a conversation with yourself or write out bullet points, think it through. If you have a teleprompter, you can write out a script.

"Finally, record it. If you need to record it three times, that's fine. Then, edit it. Throw it into Camtasia and add some bells and whistles if needed."

Nicole's Top 5 Tools

Here are five tools that Nicole recommends:

- ▶ **Your smartphone.** You can—and likely already do—take it nearly everywhere.
- ▶ **Loom** is a great software for screen-capture and talking-head videos, which can be quickly shared among distributed teams.
- ▶ **Pictory** can generate video that matches your stock and comes with AI tools to speed up editing.
- ▶ **Canva** is a powerful design tool for presentations, video, and social learning.
- ▶ **Camtasia** is an affordable video editor with graphics and interactive elements.

Nicole Papaioannou Lugara, PhD, is a learning strategist and founder of Your Instructional Designer; connect with Nicole at linkedin.com/in /nicolepapaioannouphd.

Chapter 4
Best Practices for Training Videos

In this chapter, you'll learn about:
- Using familiar media elements
- Creating a clear structure
- Using creative repetition
- Uncluttering content
- Limiting each video to one objective

I've worked with thousands of learning professionals who have started making videos. Whether it's in consulting or through interaction with participants in my workshops, I often come across people who want to re-create a Hollywood blockbuster for their training department. They copy techniques from famous directors and use special effects from groundbreaking films. It's great they are so passionate about making videos, and there's nothing inherently wrong with modeling their work on other successful production techniques.

However, you need to remember that your purpose when creating training videos is not to produce blockbuster movies or create content that's creative and expressionistic—it's to help people learn. Your priorities are less about creative expression and more focused on provoking learning. That means providing content that you know they will be able to connect to existing knowledge or skills and repeating it in artful ways to support retention.

I suspect some folks will be pleased to have chapter 3 behind them because cognitive science is complex with multiple layers, and frankly not everyone geeks out about it. But understanding how people learn is important, especially when planning training videos, because it enables you to develop principles for ensuring the content supports learning. It also gives you the agility to pivot when needed to boost learning. In this chapter, I discuss five key principles of video content that effectively support learning, understanding, and retention. They draw on the theories I discussed in chapter 3, as well as professional video production best practices. The FOCUS model is a helpful way to remember these principles:

- **Familiar.** Use content elements that learners are familiar with.
- **Outline.** Craft an intentional outline that makes content easy to understand.
- **Creative repetition.** Engage in creative repetition to ensure the learning sticks.
- **Unclutter.** Remove irrelevancies from the content.
- **Single objective.** Focus your video on one task, concept, or skill.

The Familiarity Principle

As I discussed in chapter 2, people make sense of the world through their existing memories. If you describe a fabulous beach vacation, I'll draw from my LTM a memory of a fabulous vacation of my own to understand your experience. This also applies to learning. To learn new skills and concepts, you draw on prior knowledge, a principle that's important in adult learning. However, there is a downside. If the viewer does not have an appropriate experience to draw on, they will struggle to make sense of the information you present, which increases cognitive load.

To speed up comprehension and reduce cognitive load, use content elements that viewers are familiar with. To ensure all content elements are familiar, you need to know as much as possible about the viewers. Find out their basic demographics and general interests and gain a sense of why they need the video you're making. Consider their interests, experiences, and levels of expertise. One way to learn about a viewer is to create a persona (a tool I'll explore later in this chapter). As you plan your video, choose narrative elements that will resonate with the viewers, including:

- Props, people, uniforms, locations, and actions in each shot
- Language in both spoken word content and superimposed text
- Familiar sound effects
- Music that resonates with the appropriate cultures and age groups

When it comes to footage, think about the clothing your viewers will wear, such as uniforms or standards of dress. If your audience is in the medical field, should people on screen wear scrubs or lab coats? If you're in a professional setting, should people in shot wear dress slacks or blouses? Consider where you film the action. If your audience mostly works in factories, film content with a factory background they can easily relate to and make sure your props are easily associated with manufacturing. If the video will be viewed across cultures, will any visual elements seem unfamiliar. If so, can you replace them?

Think carefully about language. Professional terms and jargon can be appropriate if your audience is familiar with those terms. But if not, replace anything that won't be famliliar with words that make sense to the audience. Use words the viewers can quickly find a meaning for in their LTM. This also applies to sound effects and music. Music means different things to different people. For example, avoid '70s jazz classics if your viewers are younger unless you want to intentionally create that atmosphere.

One of the biggest challenges to using content elements your viewers are familiar with is avoiding defaults just because they appeal to you. Language is the perfect example. Having lived for long periods in Australia, Britain, and the United States, I'm constantly filtering myself to avoid using words, phrases, and sayings that are familiar in one country but not in another. The British phrase, "This is a Blue Peter moment" makes no sense in the United States, and "Monday morning quarterback" means nothing to sports fans outside America. Additionally, Brits use the word "boot" for what Americans call a car's "trunk." A "biscuit," in Britain, is what Americans call a "cookie." When you use words that viewers are not immediately familiar with, the cognitive load increases as their brains work to figure out what that word means, usually by reviewing the context. But it's all extra work for the viewers.

Marketing professionals learn about their customers by building *personas* (sometimes called "avatars"), which are fictional profiles of a typical customer. They'll draw pictures of people who represent the personas and post key statistics to help focus the brainstorming. Most people create personas in everyday life, albeit intuitively. When buying a birthday present for a loved one, you think about who they are and what they're interested in and allow that to guide your decisions. A lot of broadcasters I have worked with create a picture in their minds of their listener and then speak to them as if to an imaginary friend.

You can create a persona by jotting down your typical viewer's general demographics. Then, consider what level of education they likely have, their technical proficiency, and their purpose for watching the video. Consider their culture, especially if your video will be viewed by folks in different parts of the world. If working in a team, make sure everyone has a clear picture of your viewer. When writing your script, keep this persona in mind to ensure the words you choose are relevant to their culture and education level.

Building a Persona

Follow these guidelines to create a persona for your video:

▶ **Describe your typical viewer.** Consider general demographics, such as age and location. What is organizational culture like? What is their profession and how does it shape their approach to work, language, and social expectations?

▶ **Discover what the viewer wants from your video.** Is the typical viewer looking for a quick overview or an in-depth tutorial? Are they interested in the big picture or details?

▶ **Determine when and where they'll want your video.** When are they likely to access your video? Is it just-in-time training or something they'll review over several weeks?

▶ **Figure out the fuzzy stuff.** What does a typical day look like for the average viewer? What frustrates them? What gets them interested? What does their workplace look like? Where and when do they work?

The Outline Principle

Some training videos are little more than a stream of consciousness. I bet you've seen software videos like this. Someone hits record on Camtasia and performs a task, like how to install the driver for a new printer. As you watch them perform the task before your eyes, they offer live commentary recorded on a tinny-sounding gaming headset. They don't start with key points to watch out for, do recaps throughout the video, or use slow motion replays to emphasize key points. And, as it's stream of consciousness, they are not intentional about which words they're using. How many times do you have to watch the video, scratch you head, and then rewatch it before you understand what's happening?

Good training videos make tasks and concepts easy to understand quickly by following an intentional structure. If something is worth learning, it's worth planning a structure for teaching it. Here's how you can plan your videos to be quick and easy to understand:

1. **Start with an overview.** In the *ASTD Handbook for Workplace Learning Professionals*, Wellesley Foshay put it nicely when he wrote, "It's easier for the learner to start with a view of the forest and then go into detail on the trees." Provide an overview that explains in some form the purpose of the video in terms of what your viewers want to know. If you created a persona, this will be easy. Add relevant details such as, "We'll follow the Acme method" or "This needs to be conducted with certain tools."

2. **Finish with a summary.** Make sure you tie everything together in a short summary at the end of the video. It both reinforces the key points and helps learners tie everything up in a neat bundle. It also triggers them to reach into their LTM to retrieve that memory, which strengthens the connection to it for when they need to use it.

3. **Create a logical flow.** Think carefully about how you break down content. Determine whether it's best to teach the task in sequence or by highlighting key steps. You can make this decision by considering the viewer's persona and the content itself. If you're teaching someone how to brew a cup of coffee, will it be more helpful to show the grinding of coffee beans before adding the coffee grounds? There's no perfect answer. Test it out on some folks to get their input.

4. **Return to the overview.** When you have multiple steps in a process, make sure to refer to the overall structure as you take viewers through each step. To pick up on the forest and tree analogy, tell them where the tree is in the forest and its purpose. Relate it to other trees so that learners know how everything fits into the big picture as well as its minutiae.

5. **Use repetition.** Memory is built by the retrieval process from the LTM. When you were a kid, you learned your lines for the school play by rehearsing them. You improved your moves in a sport by practicing them with the coach. Video can't force viewers to practice what they learn, but you can stimulate retrieval, something that marketers and advertisers have done for centuries, with repetition. Ever noticed how radio ads repeat a phone number five times? That's repetition. They might make it catchy by singing the number in a jingle. Look for places within the structure that you can subtly repeat key information to trigger the viewer to think about something that's already been presented.

Creative Repetition

In the traditional classroom, the retrieval process is activated by exercises such as discussions, journal writing, role plays, games, practices, and simulations that the trainer asks the participant to do. They are functions that the learner performs and are generally aided in a classroom because a trainer says, "OK, let's do this activity." A simple video can't coerce a learner to do an activity like a trainer can in the classroom, and this is a significant pedagogic limitation of video.

I just discussed how important repetition is for building LTM, so I urge you to use that as a device in the outlines of your videos. However, if you just repeat the same scenes or words, the learner will lose interest. If they hear a key message such as, "Bend your knees when lifting heavy material" repeated as a voice-over three or four times within a three-minute training video, they will likely tune out. Their brain tells them, "I've heard this before." So simple repetition is not as good as it might seem.

One way to keep people's attention while repeating the same message is to do it differently each time. For example, in a video on presentation skills that encourages learners to speak slowly, you could include the key point as a text graphic on one occasion, a voice-over on another, and then perhaps footage of someone in an audience saying, "I just lose track when they speak too fast." You're provoking retrieval through repetition, and by doing it differently each time, you keep the viewer from tuning out.

The Unclutter Principle

When planning content for training videos, many people worry about what to put into them. They usually think, "I can't afford to miss X," and "I have to make sure we cover Y." However, what you take out of the content is more important than what you put in. As I previously discussed, your working memory simply cannot carry lots of information at any one time. The more content you throw at the viewer, the more their WM struggles to decode the message, and the more likely they are to become overwhelmed. It's all about removing fluff.

This happens to be a standard media practice that cadets learn in their first days in a newsroom. Keen to sound smart or show a good command of English, new reporters often use big words to puff themself up. However, puffed up language is difficult to decipher, so editors will ask, "Do you really need that word?" After the usual protestations, the editor will say, "Well, let's take it out and see." They take it out and find it changes nothing. "Let's leave it that way," they'll tell the cadet.

In video, you need to review not just the written script but every content element. Do you need this piece of music throughout the entire video? How about this prop in a shot? Those graphics—do they really make something easier to understand or are they repetitive? If you can remove content elements, and the substance of the message doesn't change, delete them. If there's a phrase in the script that doesn't change the message when removed, keep it out.

The task of uncluttering is not something you do on a whim. It's an intentional process, and the guiding decision point is the learning objective. For a video on brewing coffee, I should ask, "Do I really need this footage of grinding the beans to help someone understand the process of brewing coffee in a French Press?" Yes, so I'll keep it in. What about that slow dolly shot of my cool coffee mug? No—it doesn't change the message or add to it, so I should leave it out. Thinking about how to identify what to remove leads me to the final principle for effective video: the single objective.

Single Objective

Every training video should have one objective that focuses the content and allows you to make smart decisions about what you need to include and exclude. Of course, it might be different if you're producing a series of one-hour documentaries, but for training videos, which are likely to be between 30 seconds and six minutes in length, including more than one objective will make the content confusing and editorial decisions difficult. I'll get into more detail about how to write objectives in chapter 12. What's important here is that you limit the objectives to one per video.

It's easy to think of the objective as a goal, but it's much more than that. It is a critical tool for reducing cognitive load. Every time you think of a sequence of shots, you should ask if they help achieve the objective. When you add an additional story or information, you need to ask, "Does this help the learner better understand the task?" If you have to balance two objectives when making editorial decisions, you'll never have clarity in the final product.

Often, you'll be presented with a terminal objective that has several enabling objectives. For example, changing a car tire on the side of the road is a terminal objective that includes a series of enabling objectives, such as safely parking in the shoulder, positioning the jack correctly, jacking the car, loosening lug nuts, and swapping out the wheels. Depending on the complexity of the task, it makes sense to create one video for each objective; that is, separate videos for the terminal objective and each enabling objective. This process reflects the segmenting principle (chapter 3) and may be done by creating one video with a chapter for each objective or individual video files with activities between them.

What Does All This Mean?

The FOCUS model is a convenient tool for remembering the five key principles of engaging video content:

- Use content elements that your learners are familiar with.
- Create a clear structure so tasks are shown in an organized way that makes them easy to understand quickly.
- Repeat key elements of the task, although repeat those elements differently each time to maintain visual engagement.
- Unclutter content by removing irrelevant information.
- Focus your video on one objective.

Remember, what you do in the content should also be consistent with other learning strategies you employ beyond the video itself, such as performance support tools—like checklists, process guides, and FAQs.

PART 2
KEEPING EYEBALLS ON YOUR VIDEO

The most important element in a video is what people see—the pictures. Seasoned TV professionals will tell you that video is a show-don't-tell modality. Viewers will remember more of what you show them than what you say. So, the decisions you make about the pictures—what you show, how you show it, and in what sequence you show them—are the most important you will make while producing your video.

It's easy to think that video is simply a matter of aiming your smartphone at the action, hitting record, and then clicking the stop button when the action has finished. But there's a lot more to making an intentional video that powerfully conveys a message and helps people learn. Here are some things to consider:

- ▶ How video and all its elements work as a series of message layers
- ▶ How to frame each individual shot so it powerfully carries your message
- ▶ What pictures to use and in what order to effectively convey meaning
- ▶ How to structure the overall package so it's easy to understand quickly

In part 2, I explore each of these issues and discuss how to keep viewers visually engaged. In other words, what to do to keep their eyeballs glued to the screen.

Chapter 5
Show, Don't Tell

In this chapter, you'll learn about:
- Video and the multimodal principle
- How every picture tells a story
- Video as a series of message layers
- The videographer's mindset

Hours and energy are often wasted making video. I'm not even talking about poorly produced video with shaky camera work, excessive camera moves (like unnecessarily zooming in and out), and muffled or distant audio. A lot of well-produced video that looks slick, is well lit, and sounds great unfortunately represents a waste of time and energy. You see, many training videos are produced on topics that simply don't work *visually*. As I explore in this chapter, video is a visual modality that carries most of its information in pictures, and the key to producing video that keeps people watching is to follow a *show-don't-tell* mindset.

Because video is a visual modality, training videos work well if you're showing folks how to change the toner in a laser printer, safely lift a box in a warehouse, or use nonthreatening body language. Its visual nature makes it good for conveying emotions, such as with a facial expression through a close-up shot of someone's eyes, and concepts like size and scope, such as a wide shot of a university campus. But video struggles to explain abstract ideas like monetary theory, complex concepts such as DNA coding, detailed languages like C++, or policy information like HR procedures.

None of this is new. TV, which is where news and documentaries have their natural home, has struggled to convey information about nonvisual topics like finance that relate to abstract, rather than concrete ideas. How many times have you watched a TV news broadcast for information about tomorrow's weather or the S&P 500, only to quickly forget the data moments after hearing it? We tend to forget what we hear and remember what we see. Because of this, the TV industry has developed clever ways to compensate for this, such as adding graphics.

It all leads to an important principle. Video is not the most effective modality for every training topic. For many, it represents a waste of time and money no matter how well it is produced.

The Multimodal Principle

To make sense of this we'll explore what I call the *multimodal principle,* which assumes that different modalities (audio, video, text, and graphics) have different strengths and weaknesses. When choosing what to use for instructional design, you should use the one that best suits the task you want to teach.

Let's start with some definitions. People often use the term *multimedia* to describe audio, video, text, and graphics. For fear of stating the obvious, *multimedia* is a combination of the prefix *multi,* meaning multiple, and *media.* But video—like audio, text, and graphics—is a modality, not a medium. TV is a medium that broadcasts the video modality via radio waves. Radio is a medium that broadcasts the audio modality. Print (newspapers, books, and magazines) refers to paper with ink that carries text and sometimes graphics.

Until the World Wide Web came along, each of the four modalities (audio, video, text, and graphics) basically existed on their own mediums. You couldn't show video in the newspaper, for example. If a newspaper wanted to run a story about an airplane crash, it had to do so with the written word, which takes longer to read than a watching five-second video of the crash. On the other hand, while video was good for showing the crash, it wasn't so helpful when providing details like how many people were injured, what airplane was involved, what cause was suspected, and so forth. So, the actual details were hard to convey. Because of this separation, the three modalities existed on their own and all sorts of narrative tricks existed to make up for their shortfalls. For example, TV started to develop sophisticated graphics.

The revolution came when the web created a space (not a medium) where all four modalities could exist together. I know this may seem like an esoteric conversation, but, in terms of media history, it is profound. If you were a TV news broadcaster, you only had video to get your message across; even if the topic wasn't visual, like finance, you still had to use video. You had to develop work-arounds and your story on currency fluctuations would never be as effective as it could be in print, nor could it have the same impact a story about an earthquake, fire, or car wreck might have on TV. However, different modalities can be mixed on the web, allowing you to choose the modality that best suits the topic. The overall experience becomes much more immersive. When elements of a story are visual, you can use video. When facts and specific details are necessary, text or graphics can enrich the experience.

All this parallels learning. Some topics, or parts of a topic, will be best conveyed as text or graphics, while others, such as audio, work as a podcast. This principle also releases you from trying to use video for content that doesn't work visually.

The multimodal principle accepts that each modality has its own set of strengths and weaknesses for communicating different information, so you get the most benefit from the media by choosing the most effective modality (Halls 2016b). For example, video is good when the content is about action. It's ideal for portraying psychomotor skills, like how to assemble a computer or install a modem. It's good for explaining processes, like those in nuclear power stations where learners couldn't easily see them in action. Video can draw on production techniques—such as still frames, replays, and slow motion—and emphasize elements with text graphics to reinforce key points. It's also great for providing an understanding of natural phenomena like landscapes and human emotions, and it's a faster way to convey action than text or still graphics.

However, despite these strengths, video is a weak choice for conveying topics with lots of facts and figures. It's lousy for explaining finance policy and far from ideal for conveying complex ideas, such as philosophy. Just imagine trying to create a two-minute video on existentialism— a topic that is more easily conveyed via text because the learner can reread it.

When the brain processes visual information, it does so synchronously, whereas information such as text is done sequentially. If I show you an image of a woman and her young child feeding some ducks on a pond, you see the ducks, the pond, the woman, and the child, and the action of them throwing the breadcrumbs to the ducks is decoded within a split second. However, if I explain this image in words, you need to listen until I have reached the end of my sentence before you can process the words and make sense of the scene. It is a sequential experience. The picture also conveys numerous additional elements that bog down a sentence, such as the child's age, height, hair color, clothes, and emotions. Video represents a much richer and more broad experience.

Scenes, Sequences, and Shots

Video is a visual modality that primarily communicates using the language of pictures, which is not as easy to use as it might seem because most folks are trained to communicate with words. From the moment you start school, the educational emphasis on communication is verbal, such as vocabulary choice and grammar. You write essays, answer questions in exams, and give speeches. While most people are proficient in the language of words, the language of pictures can take time to master.

Visual communication is about carefully framing what will be seen on screen, and emphasizing certain parts of an image using techniques like depth of field or camera angles. Framing a shot is as intentional an activity as choosing the perfect word in a sentence. We can be careless in word choice, as many are. But as good writers take time to choose the perfect words for sentences and structure those sentences to carry a focused message, good videographers do the same with shots and sequences.

When you write, you select words, which form sentences, which then form paragraphs. Just as words, sentences, and paragraphs are building blocks of written and verbal language, video is built on shots, sequences, and scenes:

- **Shots** are single actions or events that are recorded by a camera one at a time (Bowen and Thompson 2013a). While shots are not defined by an amount of time, they're generally understood as the action between when you press record on the camera and then hit stop. Shots are like the words you use in verbal and written communication.
- **Sequences** are series of shots that show an action unfolding (Frechette 2012). For example, a sequence could show someone picking up a telephone at their desk. Sequences are like sentences because they are like a collection of words (shots) assembled in a certain order to convey a message.
- **Scenes** are collections of sequences. For example, if someone picks up a telephone and talks with a colleague in the office, a scene might include a sequence of the person picking up the phone followed by a sequence of someone walking into the room and sitting down. And possibly a dialogue between the two people. Scenes are like paragraphs of sentences (sequences).

I will talk a lot about shots and sequences as I discuss video throughout this book because they are the visual building blocks of video. I'll also explore other visual forms of communication that you can access in video, which include graphics and special (visual) effects.

Message Layers

While video is primarily about what people see, it also includes an auditory layer made up of spoken word, sound effects, and music content. Each of these auditory forms, along with the pictures, graphics, and special effects, act as layers to carry your message (Halls 2012). While the typical viewer sees the final video as a complete whole, you can make sense of video with these layers. Because video is visual, the picture message layer is the foundational layer, and every other layer exists to either support aspects of the message that the picture struggles to convey or enrich the picture itself. Let's consider the following layers:

The Picture Layer

The picture layer refers to the shots your learner will see when they watch the video. If you're producing a video that shows staff how to use recycling bins, you might have a series of shots showing different types of waste and people putting the right waste into the right bin. The picture layer has its own set of rules, which is generally called *visual grammar*, although sometimes it's referred to as *video grammar*. These rules have evolved over the past 100 years, from the early days of cinema to TV and web video. They provide guidance on how to frame and sequence shots along with technical details like lighting and depth of field.

Pictures

Over the years, different videography terms have become widely used in different countries as well as different industries, which can get confusing. Multiple phrases can mean the same thing (like wide shot and long shot). For the sake of this book, I adopt terms that may be the same as what others use, but it helps to nail this down. For instance, I use *pictures* to broadly describe what is seen on the screen, which is most often the shots themselves.

One important presupposition in this book is that people remember more of what they see in a video than what they hear. Therefore, the picture layer plays a foundational role. Its value was perhaps captured perfectly by Alfred Hitchcock when he remarked to Francois Truffaut that "the silent pictures were the purest form of cinema" (Jones 2013). If you spend most of your time writing a nice script but forget to plan your pictures—a mistake many beginners make—you will have wasted time on the layer that is most easily forgotten. A key skill in planning pictures is drawing a storyboard, which I'll discuss in chapter 7.

The Graphics Layer

The graphics layer refers to images you create as well as any text you superimpose on a picture. Text graphics, such as captions, are also known as *lower thirds* (or Astons). For example, a TV news broadcast will have graphics in the weather forecast (like pictures of sunshine and clouds) and financial stories (such as a bar graph interspersed with text). According to award-winning media producer and former BBC executive Mhairi Campbell (2022), "Graphics can reinforce your message, add context, and deliver information quicker than a long talk or pages of text."

In the recycling video example, you could use text graphics to explain key things that are not immediately clear in the footage, such as what types of materials are recyclable, or to encourage people to think carefully about where they throw their waste. Graphics emphasize key points or illustrate things that are not always apparent in the pictures. For instance, if your video shows people working in a factory, then use a bar chart to identify how many of them have a high school diploma, bachelor's degree, or master's degree. Text graphics can be superimposed over footage or used as a standalone feature. If you're interviewing SMEs, use text captions so viewers know who the talking head is. Like the picture layer, there are specific rules that make graphics more effective.

The Visual-Effects Layer

The visual-effects layer includes tools available during postproduction. For training videos, I'm interested in three types of visual effects:

- **Transitions** refer to how one shot moves to another. Traditionally, TV editors would cut or dissolve between shots or fade to a black screen. Today, transitions are much more sophisticated and include everything from flares to barn doors, splits, cascades, blinds, and fly ins and fly outs. Transitions can be helpful narrative tools but are more often distractions. They should carry your message, so if you're creating a flashback effect, slowly dissolve to a black and white shot. If I want to create the impression of a flashback, without adding a text graphic that says, "Flashback to 1980," I could add a fuzzy dissolve transition between the shot of today's content and the shot designed to depict the 1980s.

- **Filters** can both enhance a shot or add a narrative element. Most editing software packages enable you to adjust brightness or contrast or sharpen an out of focus image with filters to enhance a poorly filmed shot. However, applying a monochrome or film grain filter to create the effect of old film can also change the feeling of a shot. Returning to the flashback example, I could add a color filter that slightly bleaches the shot to signal to the viewer it's the 1980s.

- **Manipulators** allow you to dramatically manipulate an image so that it looks very different. One such tool is chroma key— colloquially called a "green screen." If you film a person or object in front of a green screen, you'll be able to replace everything green with a new image. This effect has been used in super-hero movies, as well as to replace the outside scenery when filming in a car. Another type of manipulator is speed. You may choose to speed up or slow down the footage. If I want to show people a key psychomotor skill, such as how to correctly roll pizza dough, I could slow down the shot to highlight key hand techniques.

The Spoken-Word Layer

The spoken-word layer exists to add information that is not clear in the picture. It can include narrator commentary (like a voice-over), dialogue (such as a conversation between two or more people), or a monologue (such as a talking-head shot). Like every message layer, established conventions have emerged over the past 100 years of TV and cinema that can make spoken-word content easier to follow. (I'll explore those in chapter 12.) Spoken-word content for video does not follow the rules of written grammar. Spoken-word grammar is all about how to be understood the first time you are heard. If you watch some of the most engaging video productions in cinema, you'll notice they have surprisingly few words. That's because video is a show-don't-tell modality. In the recycling video example, I might prefer a voice-over rather than text graphics to convey information that was not immediately clear in the footage, such as what items go in the recycling bin and which ones go in the waste bin.

The Music Layer

The music layer provides a powerful tool for evoking emotion, influencing energy levels, and adding scenery. Unfortunately, music is often added to training videos without much thought. If you want to create a mood of excitement or fear, music is one of the most effective tools you have. Just think of your favorite spy movie—a serious, almost foreboding soundtrack, coupled with darkly lit scenes can keep viewers on the edge of their seats for many minutes.

Music manipulates energy too. Spas all over the world play gentle, calming music to prepare their clients for relaxation, and, in video, we can do the opposite by increasing engagement with upbeat energetic music. Music also has the power to create scenery. If you hear Jack Norworth and Albert Von Tilzer's famous song, "Take Me Out to the Ball Game," which is sung by fans at virtually every baseball game, you are immediately transported to the ball park. Hear an organ, and you might be transported to a cathedral or haunted castle. And carousel music can make you feel like you're at the state fair.

By varying when and where you use music, or add silence during the video, you can keep engagement levels high. To encourage people to recycle, I might use inspirational background music with a positive tone so that folks think recycling is a good thing.

The Sound-Effects Layer

The sound-effects layer is probably the most underused in training videos. In TV and cinema production, editors add action sound effects—like closing a car door—to video. When you film this shot on a camera, its microphone is likely to be more than 5 feet away from the car door, which means it also captures distracting ambience, such as an echo or other noises in the area like people talking or another car driving by. If you add the specific sound effect of the door closing, which was captured separately by a microphone within a foot of the sound, it will be more realistic. In the recycling example, I could add sound effects to the footage of people throwing waste into the bin to give it a realistic feeling. Sound effects also help draw attention. In TV production, a whoosh sound is often used when flying a text graphic onto a screen or when the camera does a crash zoom. If the recycling video only had text graphics and no voice-over, I could add a whoosh sound every time the graphics come on screen to draw attention to the text.

◄◄ ❚❚ ►►

If you plan your video content by thinking through each of these layers, in this order, you won't just speed up the process, but you'll also reduce mistakes and keep the content at a consistently high standard. (I'll review a rapid media workflow based on this sequence in part 4.) For example, you might want to teach someone how to set up a new account for a bank customer. Once you have broken this task into steps, created a structure for the video—which might include an overview of what's involved, individual steps such as checking the customer's ID, and entering information into a computer program—and outlined a high-level summary, you'll need to think about how you will show these steps as a video. The key principle of message layers is to start by planning the pictures, packing them with as much information as possible. If the pictures are clear and you don't need a voice-over, there's no need to include one. Likewise, if the action is demonstrated clearly without slow motion, there's no need for that visual effect.

Is Video the Right Modality?

Before investing time and energy into producing a training video, consider if it is the most effective modality for learners to understand the topic. If not, pick something different. A simple way to determine the best modality is to consider how you would teach the topic in a classroom:

- **If you would demonstrate a task when teaching it in a class-room, opt for video.** For example, if you're showing participants how to lay rebar before pouring concrete on a worksite or how to refuel an aircraft, then video makes sense.
- **If you would explain a concept, use text.** When people need to read the information at their own pace and reread it for clarity, text makes sense. For example, if you're describing tax policy, detailed HR processes, or computer programming, use text.
- **If you would tell a story or share a case study, use audio.** For example, if you're narrating success stories, history, cultural topics, or case studies, then audio is ideal.
- **If you would provide a high-level overview of a topic or show relationships between different parties, use graphics.** For example, if you need to immediately convey a situation or sense of realism, use photographs. A step-by-step process, like entering information into a customer relationship management database, could be captured as an infographic. If you're showing how far apart people need to stand during social distancing, a photograph may be best.

While thinking about content in this way can strengthen the narrative experience, it also helps you save money because it prevents you from investing in video content that won't pack the same punch as another modality. Well-produced video takes two to four hours of production for every final minute of polished video, which means you'll invest a day for every two minutes of final video. Don't waste this time if it's more effective (and consequently quicker) to use audio, graphics, or text. Think of the previous classroom question as a rule of thumb to guide decision making, but you should also consider budget, time, and individual content elements.

The Videographer's Mindset

As I have discussed, video is a visual modality. The key to successfully producing engaging video is adopting a show-don't-tell mindset, which translates into some specific practices that also draw on the psychological elements from previous chapters. Here are some key things to remember:

- Once you have analyzed and created a structure for the task you will teach in the training video, plan the pictures before you write a script. It will feel counter-intuitive until you have tried it a few times, but it almost always leads to more visually engaging content. Rather than finding pictures to fit to the words (which is difficult), you are finding words to support the pictures.
- When you brainstorm which pictures will best teach your viewers the task in your video, put yourself in their shoes. What images will speak to them most strongly? This is why developing a viewer persona is so important.
- When planning the video with the message layers approach, only use the elements that will add value. If you can get away with showing only pictures, feel free to forget voice-overs and fancy graphics. You don't need your videos to look like TV productions. You need them to show folks how to perform tasks.

In the next chapter, I'll explore the key principles of visual grammar and rules that will help you craft videos that are easy to understand.

What Does All This Mean?

The multimodal principle suggests you use a modality that most suits the topic. Video is good for action. Podcasts work well for story and narrative learning. Graphics support snapshots and conceptual overviews, while a detailed analysis is best portrayed as text. Simply ask, "Would I show this in a classroom if I was teaching people, or would I explain it, tell a story, or provide an overview?" Video is not the ideal modality for every subject, and it's important to critically review the content to ensure you're not spending time and energy producing something that might be better suited to a podcast or infographic. Unless I am providing a demonstration, there's good reason to question if video is the best modality. If it is the right modality, it's important to focus on what you will show rather than what you will say because every picture tells a story. Remember, pictures are the foundation of video, and every other element—like music, sound effects, narration, and special effects—is built on the pictures.

How to Use AI and Animation to Support Engagement

WITH GARY LIPKOWITZ

Key takeaways:
- Effective training videos are "engagement engines."
- Animated videos save time and money and offer flexibility.
- AI is supercharging everything.

Imagine a world where a learning designer can punch, "How to scan a customer's credit card," into an app, and within a few moments, the app creates an animated video—complete with characters, relevant backgrounds, and dialogue. According to Vyond CEO Gary Lipkowitz, that reality is now. And he should know. The award-winning TV producer, who has directed English language adaptations of more than 20 anime films, is leading Vyond on that path, launching key AI tools that allow learning designers to craft animated training videos faster and easier than ever.

Why Are Videos Good for Training?

"If produced correctly, the role of video is as an engagement engine," Gary explains. A lot of learners walk into training and think it will be painful. But he suggests that "you can win that battle by saying, 'This is going to be fun.'"

When asked what "correctly produced" means, Gary pivots to film language, saying, "An adaptation process needs to happen" (referring to the Hollywood process of adapting a novel into a screenplay). Like film adaptations come from pages of a novel, he says, "training videos come out of course outlines. But the videos often seem to be just copied and pasted out of the course outline—and that is not engaging."

"In a novel, you can talk about a character's thoughts, but in a video, you cannot. Yes, you can linger on a close-up and have a voice-over narration about their internal monologue, but you're back to glorified print because you're just throwing words at people. For video, you need to think about what's visual, what has movement," he says, harking back to the need for engagement. "And you need a story with a change agent and change resistor—the protagonist and antagonist—to make it engaging."

Creating Engaging Video Content

Gary says good videos start with a *treatment*—which "describes how you are going to make this an engaging video. It's your concept. Your approach. And it's less than a page. You use it to write your script, which explains what's going to happen in the video."

Complex content needs to be simplified. He uses a rubber mallet metaphor, saying you need to take your initial outline outside and break it down into small chunks. "Course outlines can be very dense, and dense is bad for learners because it overloads their cache, their system. Learners have a limit on how much new information they can absorb. Otherwise, they forget or get fatigued, and it's not encoded." He encourages folks to break the content down several times to remove all unnecessary information and ensure it's not dense.

Animated Video

Of course, these are fundamental principles for any video, whether filmed on camera or created with animation software. But Gary argues that animated video is easier to create because it gives producers more tools. "You can abstract away from unnecessary information," he suggests, while pointing at the bookcase behind me as we talk over Zoom. If the bookcase isn't germane to the message, you don't need to draw it in.

He also says, "The difference between using animated characters and live actors is night and day. Many actors in a corporate video haven't worked in that role or industry." He explains that actors need to get into the spirit of their on-screen character's context, so "they'll say the lines, but body language, temperature, and position will never be quite natural." However, he says, "We have a preset in our brains with animated TV—it's easy TV. Animated 2D characters are not supposed to be real people," so they'll never be expected to act natural.

Animated video also costs less to produce and has less preproduction and production complexity. It's easier to update and allows you to visualize ideas at any scale, including those that are tricky to capture on camera.

The Future

But, back to the future. "AI is going to supercharge what we do," Gary says. "It already solves the blank page problem." Vyond's product, he explains, "can kick-start a content outline—you can actually say, 'Make me a video about X.' Give it some parameters—your industry, audience, and that sort of thing—and it will create a script and rough cut video almost instantly. You can then adjust its tone and things like that."

I'm somewhat blown away because he suggests we upload the audio of our Zoom interview into Vyond. "We have a talk show template—great set. It will turn our conversation into a chat show." (And as a former talk show host, I might just try that.)

AI already creates visual assets for use in animated videos that can be customized to industry and style, and options like text-to-speech generators continue to improve in quality. These technologies help learning designers make more meaningful content to help people and organizations perform better. But, one thing won't change. In Gary's words, video needs to be "produced correctly." Start with a treatment, break it down so it's not dense, and make it engaging.

Gary Lipkowitz is CEO at Vyond, which is an AI-powered video creation platform; connect with Gary at linkedin.com/in/lipko.

Chapter 6
Visual Grammar

In this chapter, you'll learn about:
- The purpose of visual grammar for training videos
- Key principles of visual grammar
- General visual conventions like shot sizes, composition, and camera angles and positions

Mention the word *grammar,* and some folks run for the hills. I think it sparks nightmares of that grumpy English teacher who admonished them about incorrectly mixing tenses or a colleague who criticized a report because it wasn't written in the active voice. Grammar for many is synonymous with rules, and for some it's a bunch of rules for the sake of having rules. Unfortunately, this opinion obscures the fact that grammar is about writing more efficiently and composing content that's easier to understand quickly.

So, it wouldn't surprise me if some folks want to skip this chapter. But here's the thing: Knowing visual grammar will help you plan more engaging video content faster. Your videos will also look polished and more professional. While the term *visual grammar* is loosely used across disciplines, film and TV professionals use it to refer to filming and editing conventions that make content more engaging and easier to understand. The principles have evolved since the start of cinema through TV and web video as directors and producers experimented with the medium, playing with everything from how people look on screen to where to place objects in relation to other objects and how to plan lighting and even move the camera.

General Principles of Visual Grammar

Before getting into technical jargon, let's take a moment to discuss four key principles of visual grammar to consider when planning training videos.

The Camera's Role: The Viewer's Eye

While your camera is simply an electronic instrument attached to a lens, in a more profound sense, it represents your viewer. Where you put the camera is where you will put the viewer. If you position the camera close enough to someone that their facial expression dominates the whole frame, showing the lines around their eyes tighten as they smile, you are literally positioning the viewer a few feet away from that person. If you're filming a close-up of a technician's fingers installing memory into a desktop computer, you're literally having the viewer lean in close to peer at the memory board.

As you plan your videos, it can be helpful to think about where the learner needs to stand or sit to see the task being performed, not where to put the camera. Does the learner need to peer into a computer case or stand on the other side of the room? Would you ask learners to stand back to see the whole process? Or to step closer to see a specific operation? Different tasks require different positions. In cinema, the decision on camera placement is often made by selecting the most creative shot. While I'm not against creativity, the decision for training videos should be made by asking, "What's the best position to see the task?" Creativity comes after this decision.

Principle of Change

A key challenge all videographers face is keeping viewers' eyeballs on the screen. Professional producers use an effective method that is based on what I call the *principle of change*, which involves constantly changing shots (Halls 2016c). The reason engaging video keeps our attention is because we're drawn to change, which is inherent in action.

Humans are drawn to anything that changes. In evolutionary psychology, change represents a threat to homeostasis. Humans are safe when everything is in balance, but if something changes, that balance is threatened. If someone sitting in an outdoor café hears a car skidding around the corner, it interrupts their peaceful moment. Their head snaps up to see what's happened and whether they need to jump up and rush out of the way. And it's not just humans. If a cat is napping on a lounge, breathing slowly, and someone walks into the room, its ears will immediately perk up to gauge whether that sound is a threat. If not, it can curl back up and fall asleep. If it's an unpredictable noise, the cat will lift its head and look around. If threatened, it will quickly jump up and run to some hideaway. I call this the universal principle of change because anytime someone perceives change, they increase their attention.

That's why people get bored by slide decks with voice-overs but keep their eyes on a TV show. Any movement in the frame will generally draw attention. If you sit in an airport bar, you'll see people in conversation, looking not at their partner but at the TV screen over their head. So, when planning video content, think about how to keep action in each shot. For example, if you are filming a wide shot of the front of your office building, make sure to include people walking around to keep the content visually engaging. If you are teaching someone how to use a piece of equipment, don't start with a still image of the equipment; instead, start with a shot showing people using the equipment.

But what if there's no action? In that case, you need to create change, which is something TV news crews do every day at press conferences by changing the camera position or angle. People quickly lose interest with someone talking for more than 10 to 15 seconds, just like they do with training videos that simply feature a talking head. So, news editors will cut from the politician behind the podium to a wide shot of the journalists in the press room while the politician continues to talk. Then, they'll cut back to the podium for a moment before then cutting to a close-up of a journalist writing notes in a note pad. This constant change tricks the viewer's brain into thinking they'll miss out on something unless they stay engaged.

Less Boring Talking Heads

The most common question I've gotten at conferences and workshops over the past decade is how to make talking-head videos more interesting. My answer has always been that you can't. However, you can make them less boring.

Talking-head videos rely on spoken words to convey the content, and we know people forget more of what they hear than of what they see. But sometimes there's no choice. Talking-head videos are cheaper to produce, your boss may mandate this style, or you simply don't have time to shoot another style.

So, how can you make talking-head videos less boring? Here are some tips:

▶ **Crop in and out.** This is not an elegant solution, but it works in a pinch. If you have one wide shot, crop in and out of it every 20 seconds or so. That means cropping to a mid-shot for 20 seconds before coming back to the wide shot. Every shot change helps keep things visually interesting. The downside is that the resolution for the cropped shots is lower, but the movement is more important to promote visual engagement.

▶ **Film with two cameras.** If you have a second smartphone, or can borrow someone else's, position two cameras when filming so you can cut between both shots to increase engagement. You can also crop in and out. When setting up the cameras, position them at least 30 degrees apart. (See the 30-degree rule in chapter 8.) Editing software packages are increasingly offering artificial intelligence (AI) options that speed up the editing of two-camera projects to increase efficiency.

▶ **Use cut away text graphics.** Create text graphics of key points and cut to them while the speaker is talking. This is not the same as simply superimposing text over the picture, which is not ideal because it is harder to read and not always accessible. (I talk about how to craft text graphics so they're readable in chapter 7.) Cutting between text graphics and shots of the speaker can offer a more stimulating viewing experience.

- ▶ **Add B-roll.** To make the talking-head video more interesting, insert B-roll footage that shows what the speaker is talking about. If they're explaining a farming technique, show some video of that technique. If you can't film the footage yourself, see if you can grab it from a stock library. Many stock libraries offer subscriptions, allowing you to download footage from extensive collections.

- ▶ **Create chapters.** Review the talking-head video and create chapters so viewers can skip parts that are not relevant to them and find elements that are. (Increasingly, AI tools within video editing software can help you with this.) Add a text graphic at the beginning of each chapter so people can see what it's about as they scroll through it.

Principle of Incompleteness

My wife loves jigsaw puzzles and often exchanges them with friends. She has a spring in her step when a friend shares a 1,000-piece puzzle for her to finish on a long weekend. If we have guests, they are inextricably drawn to the puzzle table and start rummaging in the box for pieces to finish the puzzle. Most humans have an innate sense of needing completeness. A literary author takes advantage of this principle in their novel's first lines so you feel compelled to read 15 chapters to find out what happens. TV producers also use the principle of incompleteness—I was drawn into Kevin Costner's *Yellowstone* series by the cliffhanger at the end of each episode, despite the graphic violence it depicts that does not sit well with me. I had to see the next episode anyway. Same for Julian Fellowes's *Downton Abbey*—every episode left the story hanging.

When framing shots in a video, a degree of incompleteness is unsettling, and viewers want it to be completed. Symmetrical composition, such as centering people on the screen, will draw less attention because people will look at it and say, "Oh, it's complete," checking a virtual box in their mind and moving to their next interest. This is why the rule of thirds, a technique I explore later in this chapter, is so powerful. When something is out of place, it will bother viewers, intrigue them, or draw them closer.

They'll want to see it concluded. When you plan your videos, avoid making them perfectly symmetrical. Leave something incomplete. When crafting your narrative, never give the whole picture away; keep people waiting for an answer.

Hide the Technique

One of the cool things about video production is you can add special effects to enrich your message. You can use slow motion, do close-ups, or craft freeze frames. You can add special effects with chroma key and plan interesting camera angles. However, as it is with any creative pursuit, the power of the technique lies in it being invisible. Just because you have a barn-door transition or starbursts or flares in your editing software, that is not a reason to use them. Technique allows your messages stand strong, so when you overuse effects, like transitions, the viewer is distracted from the task you're showing. As you look at each of the conventions in this chapter, avoid starting with the question, "How can I put my new drone to use with a bird's-eye shot?" Instead, start by identifying what you need to show, and then go hunt for the appropriate tool or technique to show it. If the viewer notices your technique, you've lost the game.

Follow these four visual grammar principles and you'll make the best of the general visual conventions discussed in this chapter.

Shot Sizes

You have probably heard people in the biz talk about filming a wide shot or close-up. These standard terms describe how close or far away the viewer (camera) is from the person or object in shot. They are known as shot sizes, which sit on a spectrum between close-ups (showing intimacy and detail) and wide shots (showing context). In Tables 6-1 and 6-2, you'll find each term, what it means, and an example. Table 6-1 shows shot sizes for filming with a camera or drawing people with animated video software, such as Vyond.

Table 6-1. Shot Sizes for Optical-Sequence Video

Shot Size and Example

Extreme Wide Shot (XWS)

- Because it's generally used at the start of a video package to establish where the action in the video takes place, the XWS is known as an "establishing shot." It provides viewers a broad overview of where they are.
- It's also known as a "very long shot" (VLS). There is little personal information or specific detail.
- The XWS is all about context. Use it to establish the scene or at the beginning of your video.

Wide Shot (WS)

- The wide shot is also a context shot but usually shows a person from head to toe. It is not close enough to see emotions, although you can see general body language. It is also used for establishing shots.
- Use the WS to introduce a person or character and show their body language, or use it to show a whole object, such as a smartphone or forklift.

Mid-Shot (MS)

- The mid-shot is a balance of context and intimacy. While you see the person and their body language, you also see their face and emotions. In training videos, the mid shot is a terrific option because it shows what people would see if they were standing 3 or 4 feet away from someone. It is a very natural shot.
- Use the MS for interviews with SMEs or for showing parts of an object.

Table 6-1. (Cont)

Shot Size and Example

Mid-Close-Up (MCU) Shot

- The MCU brings the viewer closer to the person's emotions. It shows how people feel as the context around them starts to melt away.
- Generally, the MCU and MS are the most comfortable shots to use in training videos because people don't physically position themselves any closer to other people than they would with the MCU.
- Use the MCU when you want to show general emotions with some context.

Close-Up (CU) Shot

- The close-up represents the point where context is almost gone. This shot is all about emotion or detail. It is not a natural shot because people don't usually get close enough to other people to see these details.
- It works well in cinema and TV dramas because a lot of the messaging is around emotions. However, this is less true of training videos.
- Avoid using the close-up for people; instead, use it for objects, like turning a door handle or soldering a microchip on a circuit board.

Extreme Close-Up (XCU) Shot

- This shot is obscenely close to the subject and very unnatural. No one gets their face this close to another person in a physical setting. It is unflattering because it exposes skin imperfections and can undermine the confidence of the subject. I call this the "in your face shot" and recommend you have a very good narrative reason to use, if you choose to use it at all.
- Use it on the rarest of occasions and only for objects when you need a macro shot.

Shot sizes aren't just relevant for optical-sequence videos. When planning videos that show people how to use software, understanding shot sizes can save you time and lead to a more intentional training video. Table 6-2 shows shots for using screen-capture software to record training videos.

Table 6-2. Shot Sizes for Screen-Capture Videos

Shot Size and Example
Extreme Wide Shot (XWS)   • XWS screen captures show the whole computer screen.   • This shot is ideal for the start of your video to set the scene by demonstrating how to open the software.
Mid-Shot (MS)   • MS screen captures are close enough to show action without removing context from the shot. This shot is close enough to see mouse movements but far enough out to see the action.   • Use the MS when you want to show the software while you demonstrate a task, such as moving the mouse from one side of the screen to the other. It's also good for showing where menu functions are located.
Close-Up (CU) Shot   • This shot shows specific actions and details such as drop-down menus or specific buttons on the screen that the viewer needs to click on.   • Use the CU to show broad menu functions that are not easy to see in a mid-shot.

Table 6-2. (Cont)

Shot Size and Example
Extreme Close-Up (XCU) Shot • This shot is similar to a macro shot in still photography in which the focus is on a specific sub-action, such as content within a dialogue box. • Use the XCU to show specific menu functions within a larger menu.

Camera Angles

Camera angle refers to the vertical position of the camera, specifically whether it looks up or down at a subject or object. There are four main camera angles used in video production: low angle, eye level, high angle, and bird's eye (Table 6-3). You can use camera angles as a narrative tool to determine who has the power in the shot.

Table 6-3. Camera Angles for Optical-Sequence Video

Camera Angle and Example
Low Angle: **The Power Shot** • I call the low-angle shot the "power shot" because it gives power to the person or object in shot. It's simple psychology because you are looking up at someone. You can use it to subtly convey that the person in the shot has authority, such as in a leadership training video. • Use it to show SMEs or to indicate who is the boss in a role play.

Table 6-3. (Cont)

Camera Angle and Example

Eye Level:
The Conversational Shot

- The old saying, "We see eye to eye," conveys a sense of equality, and that idea is at the heart of this shot. Eye-level shots are conversational and natural.
- When you film this shot, position the camera a little below the eyeline so you are looking up slightly, but be subtle. This is the shot that's appropriate for most training videos.
- Use it in your training videos so the subject creates a sense of rapport with viewer.

High Angle:
The Loser Shot

- The high-angle shot involves looking down at a subject or object so the viewer has the power. It creates a sense of vulnerability. It might work for showing employees making mistakes or when you want to diminish someone's presence.
- Use it when you want someone to appear as a victim or have less presence.

Bird's Eye:
The Overhead Shot

- In the overhead shot, the camera is above the action. Sometimes, this shot looks down from a physical structure, like a balcony; at other times, you might use a drone. It's an unnatural shot because people don't always look down at action like this, so use it intentionally.
- Use it to create visual interest or show the broader context of action.

One of the visual grammar principles I discussed previously was to hide the technique. If people notice your technique, you've failed because it means they're distracted from the content. Camera angles can be powerful but need to be used subtly; otherwise, they will distract viewers from your content. For example, it's easy to shoot a low-angle shot so low that it looks ridiculous, so opt for a more subtle angle.

Composition and the Rule of Thirds

The way you compose a shot—how you position objects and people—has an important impact on its power. One of the most helpful principles for framing your shot is the rule of thirds. This technique has been used for thousands of years in Greek architecture and art, as well as more recently by master photographers. (Although it was first documented in the late 18th century). There are numerous theories about why it is important, but for me, it plays into the rule of incompleteness. When framing a shot, many people's first instinct is to put the important element—such as the object you're teaching or the person who is speaking—in the center of the frame. It's neat and tidy like the example in Figure 6-1.

Figure 6-1. Subject Centered in Frame

While centering the subject might feel immediately satisfying, the rule of thirds suggests that you should instead position the important person or object slightly to the side or slightly below the middle. Lack of symmetry grabs your attention, as you can see the comparison in Figure 6-2.

Figure 6-2. Subject Centered Versus Subject Positioned to the Side

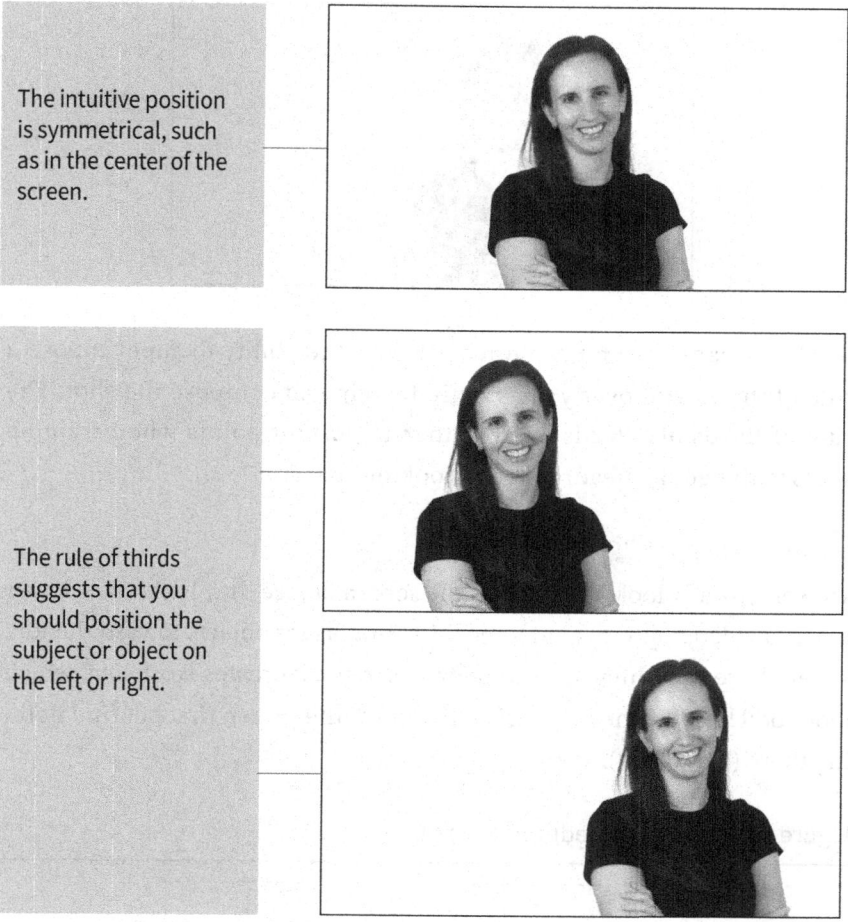

The intuitive position is symmetrical, such as in the center of the screen.

The rule of thirds suggests that you should position the subject or object on the left or right.

The rule of thirds also suggests dividing the screen into three sections, which creates three vertical and horizontal lines. The best place to position people or objects is at the intersection of those lines. In Figure 6-3, the woman is positioned along the left vertical line, and her eyes, the most important element, are positioned where the top horizontal line intersects with the left vertical line.

Figure 6-3. Subject Positioned at Rules of Thirds Intersection Points

Many cameras and camera apps have the ability to superimpose a rule of thirds grid over your picture to help you compose the shot. The rule of thirds also leads to two other important points when framing shots with people: headroom and looking space.

Headroom

Viewers usually look at the top of the screen before they look at the lower part, so videographers tend to position important objects toward the top. When there is nothing at the top of the screen, it creates *headroom*, which looks odd because viewers look at the top of the screen first but find nothing there (Figure 6-4).

Figure 6-4. Too Much Headroom in Shot

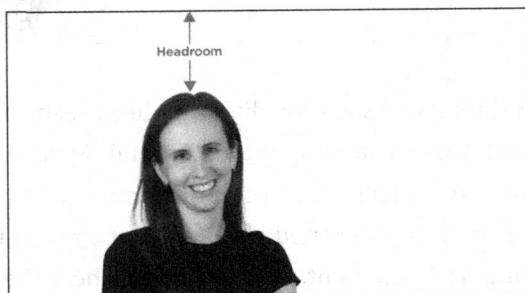

However, when you position important people or objects at the top of the screen, it looks better (Figure 6-5).

Figure 6-5. Appropriate Headroom in Shot

To avoid creating too much headroom, position the person's eyes (or an important element on an object) on the top horizontal line. Because the viewer's eyes go to the top of the screen first, this is considered important real estate.

Looking Space

In addition to headroom, the rule of thirds helps you consider the direction of the viewer's eyes with a concept called *looking space* (also called *looking room*). To create the sense that the person is looking toward the viewer, it's important to have them looking into space that exists on the screen (Figure 6-6).

Figure 6-6. Appropriate Looking Space

However, if you position the person so they are looking off the screen, you'll create the sense they are giving the viewer the cold shoulder. While this may be appropriate sometimes, it's usually important to set up each shot with the actor looking into the looking space. The shot in Figure 6-6 looks balanced because there is looking space to the woman's right, but the shot in Figure 6-7 will look off-balance if the woman is looking off screen, away from the looking space.

Figure 6-7. Not Enough Looking Space

What Does All This Mean?

Filmmakers, TV producers, and web video practitioners have learned a lot about how to use pictures to convey a message. From the silent picture days to the present, professionals have developed a series of rules known as visual grammar to guide video producers in making content that is easy to understand quickly. These rules, like English grammar, are about consistency. They guide you in how to frame each shot, where to position the camera, and how to draw the viewer in. There will be times when it makes sense to break the rules to reinforce a message, but following them will often ensure your video looks polished and professional. Visual grammar works hand in hand with key video principles, including the role of the camera, the principle of change, the rule of incompleteness, and the importance of technique being invisible.

Chapter 7
Narrative Structure

In this chapter, you'll learn about:
- The need to carefully structure content and principles to follow
- How to use narrative templates for different purposes

The human brain is an amazing thing. It sifts through information, discarding irrelevancies, to put it into an order that can be efficiently used when needed. Structure is important in most things—from the way supermarkets are laid out to the way parking lots are designed to how books are written. It's also important for training videos. To be easy to understand, they need to be more than just a stream of consciousness demonstration. They need structure.

Because there is no right or wrong way to structure a training video, it can be challenging to piece all the parts together. How should it start? What should you do to keep it interesting? In this chapter, I explore some key principles for structuring training videos to ensure they are both instructional and engaging. Then, I'll share some templates you can use or modify when crafting your own videos. They work well if copied verbatim or if used as a starting point for further innovation. In the production process, you should create the structure for your video before you draw a storyboard, which I'll discuss in the next chapter.

Key Principles

In earlier chapters, I explored how learning happens, how video as a modality conveys information, and how you can provoke learning with training videos by providing an overview that draws on a viewer's existing knowledge and experience and creatively repeating key information to encourage retention. So, how do you structure an individual training video?

Start With an Overview

People learn best by first understanding the big picture. Start by providing an overview of what learners will be able to do after watching your video so they can position each individual element of a task within the larger context. For example, if you're teaching someone how spark plugs work in a car engine, provide a high-level explanation of how a car engine works before getting into the role that the spark plugs play and any additional details like the terminal, insulator, electrodes, ribs, and other parts of the casing. If you are creating a video about the benefits of a change initiative within your organization, provide a high-level description of what the change is before espousing the benefits. In addition, before talking about how a new technology will make life easier or increase production, provide a high-level overview of what that technology does differently.

Reference the Big Picture

Regularly explain how different elements of your video relate to the big picture. Some years ago, I filed stories to a news network that had an editorial policy that required repeating the key words every 15 seconds. Because people often tune into a broadcast halfway through a story, the new audience needs a quick heads-up about what the reporter is talking about. Similarly, learners are often distracted, so you should repeatedly remind them of the big picture. It's also important to refer to the broader message while they build a schema of all the moving parts. So, if you are providing an explanation of how a spark plug works, use a wide shot of the whole spark plug before cutting to a close-up of each element.

Explain WIIFM and WIIFO

Identify the WIIFM ("what's in it for me") or the WIIFO ("what's in it for the organization"). Show viewers why this video is important to them and what they or their organization will get out of it. When viewers can clearly see the benefits, they can attach some personal meaning to it. If you have created a persona for the viewer, you should be able to identify benefits that appeal to them in the video.

Use Creative Repetition

Repeat the key points several times throughout the video, but do so using different narrative techniques. As I discussed in chapter 4, training videos are not meant to entertain, nor to make people laugh or express profound ideas. They're not art. They are a tool for instruction, so don't forget that the viewers need to engage with key elements of the content more than once to move new information in and out of the WM and LTM to support retention. This is something the learner must do; you can't do it for them. However, you can support the retrieval process by repeating key points at different times and in different ways throughout the video. For example, if you are showing viewers that they need to establish eye contact when building rapport, you might use a voice-over at one point in the video, a text graphic at another, a role play at another, and an interview with a SME at another. If you repeat the message the same way each time, the viewers will tune out, so do it differently to engage their attention.

Tackle Only One Learning Objective Per Video

Unless you're making a 30- or 60-minute documentary, multiple objectives will only elongate your content and confuse the message for the viewer. Multiple objectives will also make editorial decisions difficult because you'll be constantly wondering which objective is more important. For example, if you want to teach people how to make a cappuccino, a latte, and an espresso, create a video for each one. You don't want to worry about whether to give the coveted first 10 seconds to images of the cappuccino, latte, or espresso. You'll also be able to keep each video focused on steps that only relate to one type of coffee drink, which reduces confusion. And your viewer may only be interested in one style of coffee—why make them wade through all three types? If you have a terminal objective and several enabling objectives, consider creating one video to provide an overview for the terminal objective and separate videos for each enabling objective. Each one should reference the video about the terminal objective.

Narrative Templates

Let's put these principles into action with some sample templates. Instead of spending valuable time figuring out what comes first, second, and third in a video, templates allow you to focus on the content and be more creative. After brainstorming key elements of your content, simply drop it into a template. They are flexible, so play around with them to fit your organization's style and need. Also, consider creating several variations so you don't find yourself producing predictable videos. Or, you can try developing new templates that incorporate the principles I discussed in the previous section.

The structure is the framework. Once you structure how you'll present the content, you can then select pictures, music, effects such as slow motion, and filters like black-and-white effects or identity protection. Try not to jump ahead to planning pictures—they should be a result of your structure, not the cause. I've included a suggested amount of time to spend on each section, but think of it as a rule of thumb you can adapt to your content needs.

Explainer Formula

Helping people understand a concept is different from showing them how to perform a task. The explainer formula works well for introducing concepts, which can be tricky to convey using video and generally require more voice-overs or narration than describer videos. Table 7-1 uses the explainer video template to explain adult learning theory in a three-minute video.

Table 7-1. Explainer Video Template

Section	What	Brief Description	Percentage and Amount of Time
1	Overview	Show a concrete example of the concept. For example, if you're explaining adult learning theory, show a picture of a seminar with adults. Explain that you need to design learning experiences that appeal to adult needs.	5% 9 seconds
2	Challenge	Introduce the challenge that the video will solve. For example, show adults sitting at desks in a formal classroom looking bored with a voice-over that says, "Adults don't learn well in formal situations." Then, cut to a shot of adults reading textbooks and looking tired: "Adults don't learn best from theory."	10% 18 seconds
3	Concept	Introduce key principles using text graphics, still images, or footage with a voice-over. Finish this element by showing a text graphic listing four or fewer points that can be referred to later. For example, adults learn best when they: • Are actively engaged • Can draw on their experiences • Feel safe and respected • Have control over their learning	10% 18 seconds

Table 7-1. (Cont)

Section	What	Brief Description	Percentage and Amount of Time
4	Explain in detail	Show each element of the concept and provide text graphic support. Remember to toggle back and forth between the list you created section 3. For example, show a shot of adults walking around the room or working in groups with a voice-over that says, "Adults need to be active." Then, cut to a shot of adults discussing ideas with a voice-over that says, "Adults learn when drawing on their own experiences."	65% 117 seconds
5	Summarize	Review the key points that were listed in section 3. Use text graphics or still images.	10% 18 seconds

Describer Formula

Use the describer formula to create a classic training video that shows people how to perform a task. It's helpful for optical-sequence videos that are filmed with a video camera, animated videos, and software training videos. Start with an overview, highlight key points that viewers need to look out for, and then go through the process step-by-step while referring back to the big picture. Table 7-2 takes you through this template to demonstrate how to structure a three-minute video about scheduling an event in MS Outlook.

Table 7-2. Describer Video Template

Section	What	Brief Description	Percentage and Amount of Time
1	Overview	Show the task being performed at a high level and explain why it's important. For example, if you're demonstrating how to schedule an event in Outlook, say, "It will save you time when coordinating meetings with multiple people."	10% 18 seconds
2	Key points	Highlight anything that is important to help people perform this task such as mindsets, contexts, or background. For example, you could say, "There are multiple ways to schedule a meeting; however, in this tutorial, we'll do it from the Home tab."	10% 18 seconds
3	Overview of each step	Briefly show each step of the process. Think in terms of bullet points. This should be the first of several times in your video that the viewer sees all the steps. You can use text graphics or still shots with superimposed text on the footage. Consider revealing a list of key steps, but keep it under five points for brevity. For example, ask viewers to: • Select "Calendar." • Go to the Home tab. • Click "New Event." • Click "Add Details."	10% 18 seconds
4	Go through each step in detail	Show each step listed in section 3 in detail. This is when you might use slow-motion replays and other effects to highlight important aspects of each task, such as close-ups of buttons or key menus. Reference the list of steps so viewers know where they are in the process.	60% 98 seconds

Table 7-2. (Cont)

Section	What	Brief Description	Percentage and Amount of Time
5	Recap each step at a high level	Summarize each step at a high level to remind viewers what they need to do. Use text graphics or still images of the action shots from section 4.	10% 18 seconds

Promoter Formula

Talent development professionals may find themselves promoting new ideas, technologies, or ways of working. For example, in change management initiatives, they may be required to help staff develop awareness of the need for new technology or the need to move a corporate division to another location. The promoter template in Table 7-3 outlines a three-minute video explaining why new software is necessary to support a new supply chain.

Table 7-3. Promoter Video Template

Section	What	Brief Description	Percentage and Amount of Time
1	Challenge	Explain the challenge facing viewers. For example, a new supply chain might require the use of data points that the existing software can't provide.	20% 27 seconds
2	Discuss	Show the available options to the viewer. For example, keeping current technology means more work for staff and longer work hours spent tracking key data manually. Installing new technology will save time and allow all data to be tracked, while doing nothing means the company loses its competitive advantage.	15% 27 seconds

Table 7-3. (Cont)

Section	What	Brief Description	Percentage and Amount of Time
3	Explain	Explain more about the option being adopted. For example, the option will enable the company to collect more data, make data collection easier for staff, and allow the organization to maintain its competitive advantage. Also, explain the costs of the new technology, including downtime and need for more training, but point to the benefits.	45% 81 seconds
4	Review	Provide a recap. Repeat the key challenge and explain how the solution will benefit the viewer and their role in its implementation.	15% 27 seconds

Advertiser Formula

Often, trainers find themselves needing to advertise a service or product with a video. There are many well-known formulas you can use to structure your video; the best known is probably AIDA—attention, interest, description, action—named after Verdi's opera. It has its fair share of fans and critics, but it's a helpful way to think through how to urge someone to take action. It's also used in TV and radio ads. Table 7-4 takes you through a three-minute video advertising a class on body language.

Table 7-4. AIDA Formula Template

Section	What	Brief description	Percentage and Amount of Time
1	Attention	First, grab the viewer's attention with something that speaks to them. For example, if you're encouraging people to come to a class on body language, you might start with a role play or demo of someone totally misunderstanding body language. Perhaps you highlight the embarrassment of the misunderstanding.	5% 9 seconds
2	Interest	Once you have the viewer's attention, you need to engage them and maintain their interest. For example, help people understand that the embarrassment wouldn't have happened if the person had been able to read body language.	15% 27 seconds
3	Description	Once the viewer is interested, describe the service or product you want to sell. For example, explain that a lot of communication is nonverbal, so understanding body language will help them manage situations better. Invite them to attend a workshop on understanding body language because it will solve their problems.	60% 117 seconds
4	Action	Now that you've gained the viewer's interest and provided the information, you need to urge action. For example, provide information about how to sign up for your workshop, and urge them to do so.	15% 27 seconds

What Does All This Mean?

It's important not to leave the structure of your video to chance, nor fall into the mistake of winging it, so it ends up as nothing more than a boring and hard-to-follow stream of consciousness. It doesn't matter if you're creating an optical-sequence video or using screen recording software or animation. If you think about first providing an overview before showing a task, and then provide regular recaps while carefully leading viewers to a conclusion, you have a better chance of creating content that viewers will use. You can always plan the structure of every video from scratch, but to save time, adopt or develop narrative templates or formulas that you can drop key information into.

How to Repackage Existing Videos Into Digestible Chunks

WITH MATT GJERTSEN

Key takeaways:
- Make longer videos more engaging by dividing them into short chunks.
- Invest time to ensure each chunk is meaningful.
- Use the behavioral objective to guide editorial decisions.

Lunch & learns are a staple of organizational life and a helpful tool for knowledge management. A speaker presents a topic for 60 minutes to a group of staff, who bring their lunch and listen. But, what about staff who are out of town or attending another meeting?

Los Angeles–based training consultant Matt Gjertsen is helping clients use video to capture that knowledge and share it widely through the organization. But, doing it right involves more than just hitting record on a camera and uploading a video file.

The first five minutes of a lunch & learn recording are often dead air. "People are still coming into the room," Matt explains. What presents well with a group of people doesn't always translate to the video modality. "Delivering to a classroom means you'll repeat things a lot, but in video, you don't need to. Viewers can hit rewind and listen again."

Content Should Be Packaged to Work as Video

That's not all. Speakers often reference people sitting in the room who aren't relevant to and can't be seen by viewers watching weeks later. Speakers also joke about things in the room that don't make sense in video and often pivot their presentation midstream to answer ad hoc questions, taking more time to get back on track. Without the personal engagement of being in a room and in the flow of the event, these unedited video recordings are choppy and lack engagement.

So, Matt takes lunch & learn videos and packages them into digestible bite-sized chunks. And it shouldn't be surprising that a lot of the original recording—those awkward jokes and pauses as someone shuffles into the room or needs to fix the data projector—ends up on the cutting room floor.

"You can take what was an hour of video that no one was watching and turn it into about 15 minutes," he explains. It's also not just a whole sequential 15 minutes; rather, it's a series of shorter three-or-four-minute chunks of focused topics so that learners can watch at their own pace when they want, without having to wade through video downtime.

Workflow

Chopping longer videos into shorter pieces sounds easy, but it takes time, a process, and some discernment. "I'm probably spending five to 10 hours editing an hour of content," Matt says. Ten hours sounds right to me if I'm talking about quality video. People underestimate how time consuming video production is. So, how does he do it?

"First, get a sense of the full work," he says, noting that speakers often meander around a topic. "During the first pass, you're trying to get a sense of the structure."

But, you don't always get the structure on the first try. "Sometimes, you have to just back away and let it sit in your brain overnight," Matt says. Then, you come back and go through it again. In this second pass, you get a sense of what the key messages are. So, I start to log the whole video, noting the things that are important. On the third pass, I start to make decisions."

At this point, he identifies what to remove from the video, as he whittles it down to a cumulative 15 minutes. During the second and third passes, he'll use video tools with advanced AI functions.

Editorial Decisions

How does he know what to remove and what to leave in? "I keep coming back to the behavioral piece," Matt says as he explains his decision-making criteria. "Because of my training background, I want to know what the behavior is that people want to get out of the video. So, I use that as the lens to view the content."

Of course, behavioral objectives, or learning objectives, are a critical start for crafting any learning experience or learning asset. The clearer they are, the easier it is to determine what stays in and what goes.

Tools

"Camtasia was my first editing tool," Matt says. "It was absolutely amazing because it's really easy to learn and is powerful with lots of assets built into it." But, as his editing needs became more complex, Matt shifted to using Adobe Premiere Pro, which is exclusively a video editor and offers some helpful AI tools: "There's a plug-in I use for multicamera editing and another option that, if you tell it some basic information about video and audio feeds, basically cuts it up, removes dead time, and removes umms and stutters."

It's amazing how good technology, an understanding of the behavioral objective, and some key workflows can make engaging video that's accessible to the whole organization.

Matt Gjertsen is the founder and chief learning officer of Better Every Day Studios; connect with Matt at linkedin.com/in/matthewgjertsen.

Chapter 8
Planning the Pictures

Now that you're armed with a command of visual grammar and a narrative structure for your training video, you're ready to start planning the pictures. What footage or screen recordings will you capture to show viewers how to perform the task? How will you frame each shot? Will you use close-ups or mid-shots? Eye-level or low-angle shots? Where should you position the camera to give the viewer the impression they're close to the action? These are the questions to ask before picking up a camera, logging in to Vyond, or firing up Camtasia. I could quote the slogan "If you fail to plan, you plan to fail" and others like it, but the truth is that planning your pictures will save you time and help you consistently achieve better-quality footage. When you plan, you should think about the shots you need, how to frame them, the order in which they should be viewed (not the order they are filmed), and how they will all flow together.

In this chapter, I discuss some helpful principles to consider when framing shots. I explore them through the lens of optical-sequence videos, but these concepts also apply to screen-capture and animation videos. Once I have explored the principles of picture planning, which includes what goes into each shot and how to compose it, I'll discuss three practical tools you can use ahead of shooting: storyboards, diagrams, and shot formulas.

Video Hack: Location Scouting

While it won't always be possible, it helps to scout a location before planning your pictures for optical-sequence videos. You'll get a good understanding of the scene's aesthetic feel and can anticipate issues that might crop up during filming. Your site visit may also inspire you to think differently about your pictures. Scout the location at the same time of day that you plan to film so you'll better understand the lighting conditions (the sun will be in a different position in the morning than in the afternoon). Also, if the location is heavily trafficked and people are likely to get in your way while filming, you may want to bring a few friends to act as crowd control or enlist the help of security. During the scouting expedition, you should also review safety issues for both your crew and the actors appearing on video. Walk around the location and soak it in. Stand for a moment where the camera will be and visualize what the scene should look like for viewers.

Elements of a Shot

Novelists select every word in a sentence with intentionality. Videographers need to do the same when planning each shot. So where do you start? Folks who are intuitively visual can work through this process without much conscious thought. But for those of us who are not so inclined, it takes some planning.

The less you leave to chance when thinking through your pictures and planning your filming, the more control you will have over the final product. Picture planning should start only after you've created a structure for your video. Envision the background and how it will convey the context. Consider the people and objects, especially what they need to be doing and where they need to appear in the frame. Think about using movement to keep viewers engaged and create flow, as well as whether camera movement is necessary. Finally, imagine how visual effects may help.

There are five visual elements to consider with each of your shots:

- Background
- Objects and people
- Movement in the frame
- Movement of the camera
- Effects

Background

Your video's background provides viewers with context. That's why TV producers often film professors in front of a bookcase, scientists in a laboratory, police officers in front of a squad car, accountants behind a desk, and retail staff behind a cash register. The backdrop quickly establishes what the video is about, as well as credibility. Smart videographers also position objects to reinforce key messages. For example, authors often have a copy of their book on the bookshelf. Scientists may position a key piece of equipment within the frame. If you're teaching customers how to use certain products, put those products discreetly on display.

If you forget to plan the backdrop, you can run into problems that undermine your message by either communicating the wrong information or creating dissonance. A former retail client once filmed a demonstration in a supermarket in front of the wrong merchandise rack, which showed products they were going to stop carrying when the video was released. Another client filmed a video in a manufacturing environment but workers in the background were inadvertently operating a piece of machinery against safety standards, undermining the video's message.

Think carefully about what's behind the people or objects in the frame. Consider whether it's distracting, and, if necessary, replace it with a white screen.

Objects and People

A training video is generally focused on an object, person, or both. The object might be a tool—such as a cash register or computer software—that someone needs to use. Think carefully about the relevant part of the object. When you plan your pictures, you need to ask, "What does the viewer need to see to successfully perform this task?" Is a particular button, lever, or control especially important? Then, you need to make sure that button is prominent and easy to see.

When filming people, think about what they will wear, how they will stand, and what actions they need to perform. Generally, the most interesting part of a person in a video will be their eyes; however, if they are performing an action, it will be their hands or feet instead. Where do they look on the screen? If you're filming an action, think about whether it would be easier to follow if you used an aerial or overhead shot or a shot looking over the person's shoulder.

When you're planning to film an object or person, think about what the viewer needs to see and how to best show it. For example, showing the way someone kneads pizza dough might be best shot using a high-angle close-up. If you're showing someone how to open a truck's lift gate, a low-angle wide shot and a close-up of the person latching the gate might work best.

Movement of Objects and the Camera

Consider movement in the shot as well as how the camera moves. In the shot, think about how the actors or objects, like a vehicle, will move. Camera movement describes how the camera physically moves; for example, panning left to right or tilting up or down. Movement is critical and should be in as many shots as possible unless there is a narrative imperative against it.

As you plan the pictures, think about how an object needs to move. For example, if you're showing a conveyer belt, should it go left to right or front to back? If you're filming a person, do they walk toward the camera or away from it? Or do they come into frame from left to right?

A friend of mine who I worked with at the BBC is somewhat of a camera purist. He told me once that all camera movement should be banned. "You shouldn't need to zoom or pan if the movement within the frame is compelling enough," he said. But I think he was exaggerating to make a point. Camera moves—like panning, tilting, dollying, and zooming—are used most often when there is little movement in the frame. It's best to aim for movement in the shot rather than moving the camera. For example, if you're capturing a general view of the entrance to a company's headquarters, film it while people are walking in and out of the front doors. If no one walks in the shot, it's boring. If you're filming someone opening a door and walking through the doorway, shooting a close-up of the person's hand pulling down on the door handle will maintain interest. Avoid using still shots, which always look awkward and out of place when they're inserted between real video footage.

If you have no alternative but to show an object that doesn't move, that's when you should use camera movement. Ken Burns did this in his series *The Civil War*. He had old black-and-white photos, which are not as engaging when shown on TV, so he moved the camera to keep the action going. You'll find that when you pan or zoom into photos or still objects, people refer to this as the "Ken Burns effect." Sometimes, camera movement can have narrative value, but it's not as often as many people think. For example, if you need to create the sense of journey, you might dolly the camera through a group of people or along a road, as if driving a car.

Effects

The final consideration when planning pictures is the effects. But beware, overdoing effects can lead to what I call "video bling." Like jewelry bling, video bling, happens when the video operator pans too much without reason. It also describes zooming incessantly or transitioning between shots with distracting effects like blinds or flares. There's nothing wrong with using effects sparingly as long as they have a narrative purpose. For example, if you need to show a change in location, you might use a swipe or a pixelation transition to signal that you are shifting the viewer to another location. Just don't use special effects without being clear about their purpose.

There are many learning situations that can be helped by effects. If you're showing a psychomotor process, you may find using still effect or slow motion make the task easier to understand.

The Big Picture

So far, I've discussed the micro-level details of what goes into a shot. Now, you need to think about how it all fits together. As much as each shot needs to be framed carefully, it also needs to flow seamlessly to the next shot in a way that is not distracting. There are four considerations to remember:

- Eyeline matching
- Action flow
- Left-right balance
- Camera position

Match the Eyelines

Eyelines refer to what someone in a frame is looking at. Perhaps it's a person or even an object like a car or building. In many shots, you don't see what someone is looking at, so you should create another shot that shows the person or object they're looking at. For example, if you show two people talking, such as an interviewer and a SME, the SME will most likely be looking toward the camera, but the viewer won't see who they are looking at. To make the shot more interesting, cut to the interviewer, matching the eyeline so that each person is looking in the direction of the other when you cut between shots. Otherwise, it looks unnatural.

Eyeline matching is important for continuity and helps you see where people on screen are looking. Figure 8-1 shows how to match the eyeline in the SME interview example. In the first shot, the SME is looking at the camera and interviewer. It is reversed in the second shot so that the interviewer is looking at the SME.

Figure 8-1. Match the Eyelines

Be Consistent With Direction

Next, consider the directional flow of action. In many of your shots, people and objects (like a car or piece of machinery) will be moving in and out of the frame. Make sure that movement is consistent—if a person walks out of frame in shot 1 to camera right, the next time the viewer sees them, they should walk into the frame from camera left, as if returning to where they came from. Likewise, if a car is driving in and out of frame from left to right, when it appears in the next frame, have the driver come in from camera left to support continuity.

Balance the Shot

When including multiple people or objects in a video, position them consistently. For example, if you have two SMEs talking about an important topic, position them on the same side of the screen of the first shot they appear, every time they appear. If you have two SMEs who are expressing opposing ideas, position them on different sides of the frame (looking into the frame) every time they appear on the screen. This is a common practice in current affairs documentaries, and it makes it easier for the viewer to identify who is who as you move from shot to shot.

Political stories often have a person representing one party always appearing on the frame's left, looking into the screen, and the politician from the other party positioned on the right, looking into the space on the left side of the screen. Anytime they appear, they should be on the same side to preserve continuity.

Position the Camera

Where you place the camera can also make your video feel authentic or inauthentic. To get it right, consider where your viewer would want to be. One convention that videographers use is the *180-degree rule*, which relates to the axiom "Don't cross the line." When setting up a shot, visualize the location from above like a map and draw an imaginary line from one side to the other. This is the action line. Once you have established where this line is, position your cameras to look across it. Do not position cameras looking back over the line.

The 180-degree rule can be a tricky concept to get your head around. Imagine you're at a tennis match. Because you generally sit on one side of the court, you know which direction each player is hitting the ball. If you see the ball hit in one direction, you'll know who hit it. Sadly, because humans do not possess the ability to teleport to the other side of the court, you will only see the action from one side. The court is a line. However, if you're watching the match on TV, you'd get disoriented if the broadcast kept cutting between a camera on either side of the court—you'd likely lose track of who hit the ball because the player originally hitting to the left is now hitting to the right. The more the camera swaps from side to side, the more disorienting it will be.

To apply this principle when filming an interview with a SME, create a line between you and the SME. Keep the camera (or cameras) on only one side of that line. If you're filming a studio discussion, follow the same rule, as shown in Figure 8-2. It doesn't matter where you position your camera as long as it stays on one side of the line and looks either across it or along it. It should not look back from the other side of the line.

Figure 8-2. The 180-Degree Rule

This general rule leads to another, which is known as the *30-degree rule*. The 30-degree rule is easier to understand when editing footage. I previously discussed the need to regularly change the shot's position or angle so viewers stay engaged. To do this, you will need to film the action multiple times, placing the camera at a different location for each take. You then edit these shots together. For example, if you film a driver walking to a forklift and climbing onboard, you'll film it three times, placing the camera at a different location for each take. The 30-degree rule suggests drawing an imaginary action arc on the ground (just like you imagine the action line in the 180-degree rule) and position each camera at least 30 degrees away from the other cameras (Figure 8-3). This makes it easier to cut between shots when editing and avoid a jump cut (which I'll talk about in chapter 14).

Figure 8-3. The 30-Degree Rule

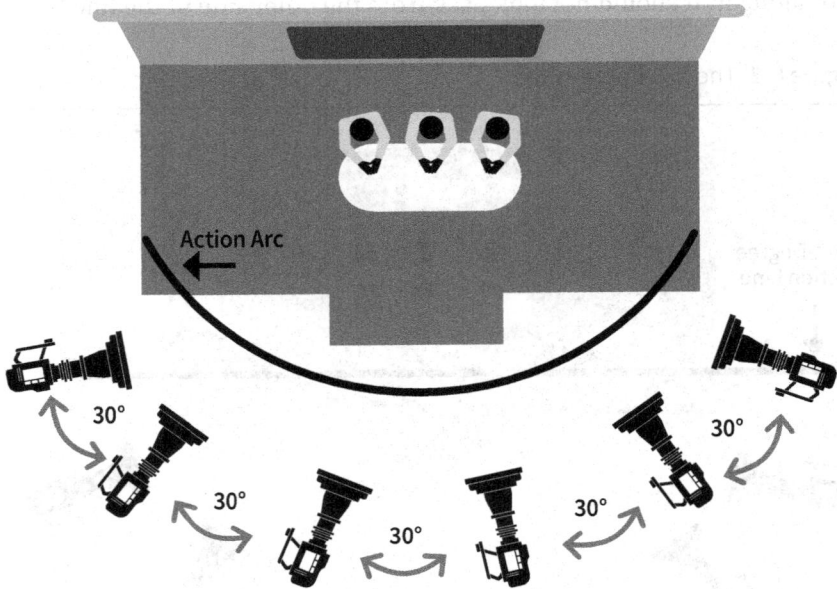

What Planning Looks Like

If you're thinking, "Gee, there's a lot to remember," you're not wrong! This is why it's important to plan your pictures before you grab a camera and go to the location you're filming. If you haven't planned the pictures, your brain will be overloaded trying to remember the key steps of filming, as well as where to position the camera, how to frame the shot, and whether the person or object should move from left to right or appear to camera right or left.

In documentary filmmaking and cinematic storytelling, producers typically draw a storyboard to set out each individual shot. They may also create a diagram that shows camera positions from an aerial perspective. Let's consider each option.

Storyboards

Storyboards are pages that show every shot you plan to film. They usually consist of a series of panels within which you map out how your shot should look. Number each panel to help you prepare your shot plan (which I'll discuss in chapter 12). You should start by drawing a rough sketch of the background—perhaps a factory if you're interviewing someone about how to safely load a forklift. You should then look at the frame, perhaps through the lens of the rule of thirds, and position the forklift at the intersection of the lower right lines. If you want to have the forklift drive, which is a good idea because it shows action, draw an arrow to show where it will go.

In addition to drawing the picture, you may choose to add some descriptive text. For example, you might write, "WS of forklift in warehouse B" below the panel. If you plan to dolly in to the forklift, you may also include that information. If you want any dialogue or commentary, you'll note that as well, although it won't be word for word. For example, you might include "V/O introduces objective." If two people are having a conversation, write, "Dialogue about safety standards." You'll map out the complete dialogue in the script that you write after crafting the storyboard.

Storyboards do not need to be pieces of art unless you're working on a high-end production or in Hollywood. For training videos, it's less important to follow the right template than it is to have an image that clearly explains what the shot should look like to everyone involved. Use stick figures and avoid shading because the storyboard will be easier to print out and distribute to stakeholders involved in the video (Figure 8-4).

Figure 8-4. The Beginning of a Storyboard

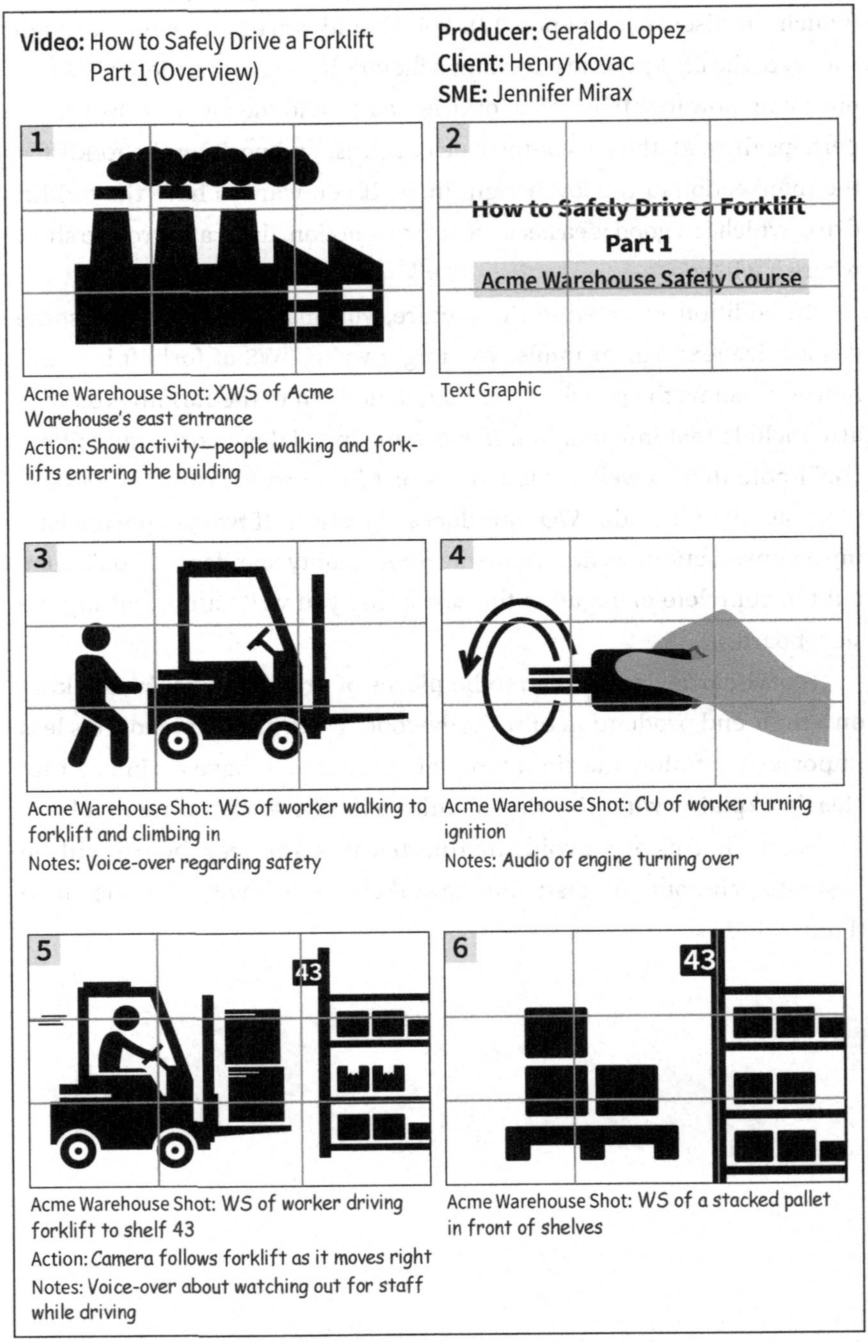

Video: How to Safely Drive a Forklift Part 1 (Overview)	**Producer:** Geraldo Lopez **Client:** Henry Kovac **SME:** Jennifer Mirax

1

Acme Warehouse Shot: XWS of Acme Warehouse's east entrance
Action: Show activity—people walking and fork-lifts entering the building

2

How to Safely Drive a Forklift
Part 1
Acme Warehouse Safety Course

Text Graphic

3

Acme Warehouse Shot: WS of worker walking to forklift and climbing in
Notes: Voice-over regarding safety

4

Acme Warehouse Shot: CU of worker turning ignition
Notes: Audio of engine turning over

5

Acme Warehouse Shot: WS of worker driving forklift to shelf 43
Action: Camera follows forklift as it moves right
Notes: Voice-over about watching out for staff while driving

6

Acme Warehouse Shot: WS of a stacked pallet in front of shelves

Storyboards can help you in several ways. First, they save time in production, taking the pressure off videographers setting up their shots. You don't want to arrive on location and waste 20 minutes trying to figure out where to the put the camera or deciding whether a high- or low-angle shot is best or whether to shoot wide or close. When you're under pressure, it's easy to make mistakes and miss key shots. I've lost count of how many folks I've seen have to go back to a location to film one or two more shots because they needed a few extra scenes to make the video seem realistic or flow smoothly. With a good storyboard, you'll have made these decisions before you arrive on location, so your focus can be on creativity and things like lighting, focus, and audio.

Additionally, storyboards enable you to visualize how everything flows. You can think about the rule of thirds, camera movement, action, and blocking the whole sequence. If you're new to video, this process will also train you to think visually. It forces you to slow down and make deliberate choices, conditioning you to think like a professional videographer.

Storyboards also help teamwork. They ensure everyone on your team knows exactly what shots are needed. Written instructions for a shot can be easily misunderstood. If you ask for a shot of a person walking through a door, you might find three people thinking of different doors from different angles. They won't know if you want a close-up on the door handle or simply a wide shot of the whole sequence. Storyboards show where the action takes place in the frame and how it flows to the next shot. They also help editors, especially those who weren't on-site during filming.

In my book *Rapid Video Development for Trainers*, I discussed the importance of creating storyboards when planning video. At conferences and workshops across the US, I invested a lot of effort encouraging people making training videos to start with a storyboard before writing a script. But my ideas were met with a lot of resistance. For some people, it just seemed to drag down the production process. "Jonathan," they'd say, "spending 20 minutes to map out each shot is a waste of time when I can make it up as I shoot." (It may seem counter-intuitive, but

I argue it's the opposite.) For other folks, the storyboard was simply a heavy lift because we are trained in school and college to communicate using words, not pictures. We are trained to write essays, not draw art, so the idea of thinking about how each shot looks rather than just what it does can feel overwhelming. And others were just not good at drawing anything more than a basic stick figure.

Now, I'd like to say that this need to start with a storyboard was my idea, but it wasn't. It was simply something I learned at the BBC, where it was widely practiced by award-winning documentary and drama producers. The good news is that the way we make training videos has matured since I started sharing the value of the storyboard. Many folks writing blogs on training videos today also suggest using storyboards.

Diagram

There will be times when a storyboard is not sufficient to convey complex camera moves or shot sequences. In these cases, you'll need to map out the action on a diagram. In professional TV and cinema, diagrams are used for complex action scenes, like car chases or choreographed fights. While training videos may not be that complex, you may need to draw a map showing how a handheld camera follows a presenter or actor demonstrating a task. For example, if you're filming a customer's journey in a retail outlet, following an actor through five stops at different spaces within the store, create a diagram (Figure 8-5). It's easier and quicker to understand than a list of written steps.

Figure 8-5. A Diagram Showing the Journey of the Camera and Actor

---

Action Diagram for Retail Journey Video
- Location: Bloomfield Office Supply Store
- Notes: Filming needs to be completed before the store opens at 8 a.m. Actor will be followed by the videographer using a gimbal.

1. Anjali walks into the store and heads to the cardstock section. She picks up a letter sized piece of yellow cardstock.
2. She then walks to the office furniture display and examines the FlexiSpot E9 desk. She reads the price tag.
3. She then walks to the printer section and picks up some Epson toner.
4. She heads to the checkout with her items.
5. She walks out of the store through the exit.

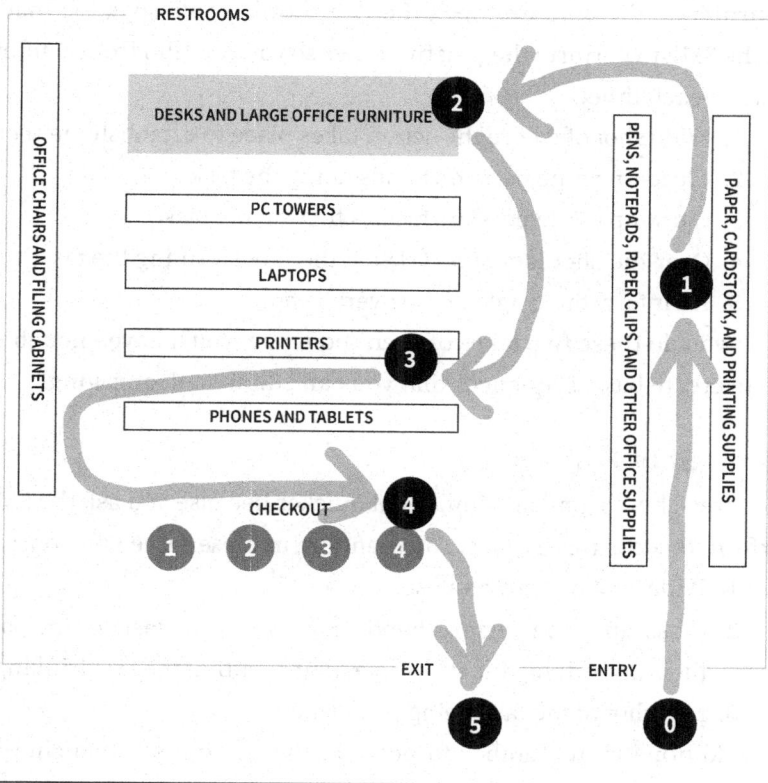

Shot Formulas

Sometimes, you can't plan for a shoot. Perhaps a key SME arrives unexpectedly in your office, so you take the opportunity to film her performing a task, such as changing the photocopier's toner. With no time to plan, what do you do? You can follow what's known as a shot formula. There are two main shot formulas to know: the five-shot formula and the three-shot formula.

Five-Shot Formula

The five-shot formula was developed by New York videographer Michael Rosenblum, and it's used by backpack journalists around the world. Returning to the SME example, the five-shot formula suggests that you ask the SME to perform the task five times so you can film from a different position each time:

1. Wide shot of where the action takes place to establish the scene
2. Close-up of the person's hands doing the task
3. Close-up of the person's face as they do the task
4. Over-the-shoulder shot (OTS) of them performing the task
5. An interesting angle of the overall shot

If you do these five takes of each sequence, you'll have enough footage to create basic sequences that you can edit to look engaging.

Three-Shot Formula

The three-shot formula is similar but quicker because you ask the SME to perform the task three times. You then film in these three positions:

1. Wide shot of the overall sequence
2. Close-up of the person's hands performing the task (or the part of their body doing the task—like their mouth if they're drinking)
3. Mid shot of the task being performed

Additionally, remember to position the camera so each shot is 30 degrees away from the others.

Text Graphics

A key element of many training videos is text graphics. As a message layer, text graphics can add specificity to a video by providing details pictures can't, such as facts, names, quotations, and other important data. Text graphics are especially important if you include information that viewers need to write down or recognize correct spelling. Richard Mayer's multimedia principles offer guidance for using graphics—such as the signaling, coherence, and spatial contiguity principles—and so do traditional TV practices.

As you consider using text graphics, remember to only use them when needed. If text graphics don't add value, don't include them. Video editing software offers many ways to add graphics, such as superimposing text on video footage. But, unless you are adding someone's name in a caption, I recommend avoiding superimposing text graphics on pictures. It is too much information for the brain to process and can cause accessibility issues. Rather, create a separate text graphic, and cut to it so the viewer only sees the text graphic.

Let's look at some specific techniques that will make your video not only easier to understand but also more professional.

Typeface

Typeface choice is an important decision because it affects how easy the text is to read as well as the general look and feel of the video. You don't want folks squinting at the screen to make sense of text that's in a cursive font or too small to read. I could talk for hours about typeface and font theory, so the only comments I'll share here are about type and size.

When choosing a typeface, I always recommend a sans-serif one (like Calibri, Arial, or Helvetica) because it looks more modern and is usually easier to read on screen (Figure 8-6). Serifs are the little hooks on the end of each character in typefaces like Times New Roman (or Source Serif Pro, which is what you're reading right now). While serifs add a traditional feel and make reading on paper easier, they often pixelate on screens. I also avoid thin fonts, which are not as easy to see.

Figure 8-6. Serif Versus Sans-Serif Typefaces

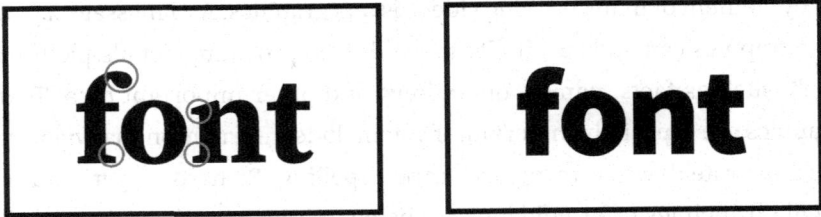

Also, avoid making text too small. I've seen a lot of videos with tiny, detailed words that are hard to read. It might look clean and tidy, but the viewer has to increase their efforts to make sense of things. You should have only 10 to 15 words on a screen, erring toward 10, and the text should fill two-thirds of the screen (Figure 8-7). Pay attention to function over form.

Figure 8-7. Comparing Font Sizes

Left-Aligned Text

When you have multiple lines of text in a text graphic, align it to the left. When reading English, you are conditioned to return your eyes to the left to find the next line. The next line should start under the beginning of the preceding line. If you use centered text, the viewer will have to expend more effort to read it because their eyes will go to the left, but they'll have to search for the start of the next line. Many people opt for centered text for aesthetic reasons. But while it looks more symmetrical, it's not easier to read. If your text is not functional and more decorative, such as a title or copyright notice at the end of the video, centered text is fine. But for instructional text, align it to the left (Figure 8-8).

Figure 8-8. Left-Aligned Versus Centered Text

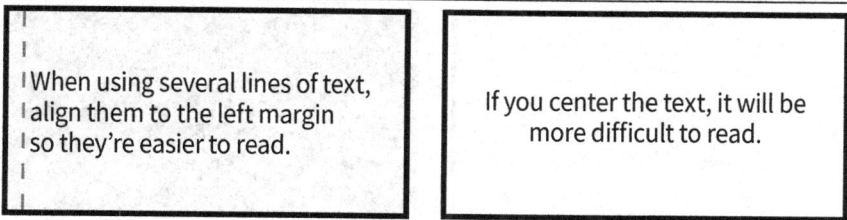

When using several lines of text, align them to the left margin so they're easier to read.	If you center the text, it will be more difficult to read.

Captions

A traditional technique used in TV to explain to viewers who is on the screen is to superimpose a caption on the lower right third of the screen. While I generally recommend against superimposing instructional text on video footage because I think it increases the viewer's cognitive effort and limits accessibility, it is appropriate for talking heads.

Take note of the background footage—if there are varying colors, your text can easily get washed out. Add a drop shadow or a colored box behind the text to ensure the caption is easy to read (Figure 8-9). I don't have an opinion on how the text graphic appears, but I usually dislike flashy, spinning graphics that distract from the message.

Figure 8-9. Creating Superimposed Captions

Contrast

Text is easier to read when it strongly contrasts with the background image. Ensure the font color is not similar to the background; otherwise, it will be hard to see (Figure 8-10).

Figure 8-10. Use Contrast to Emphasize Text

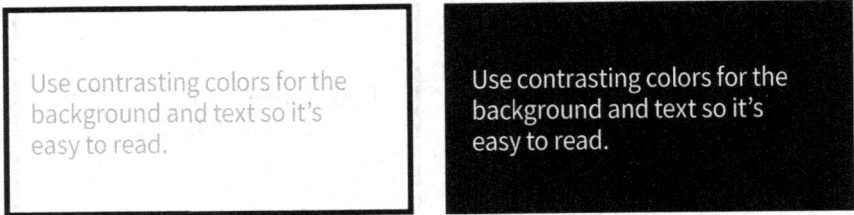

Use contrasting colors for the background and text so it's easy to read.	Use contrasting colors for the background and text so it's easy to read.

Single Idea

It's easy to cram a lot of text onto a text graphic; however, this increases cognitive load. I recommend keeping each text graphic to one point or idea. Aim to use as few words as possible, and no more than 15 per screen (Figure 8-11).

Figure 8-11. Multiple Versus One Idea in the Frame

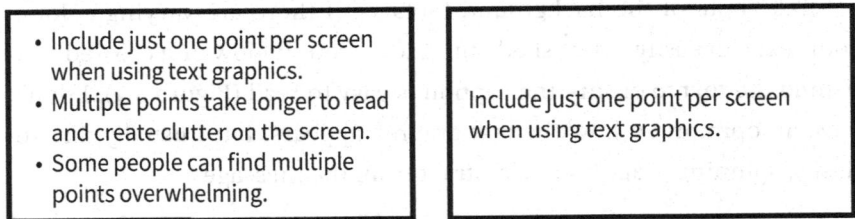

• Include just one point per screen when using text graphics. • Multiple points take longer to read and create clutter on the screen. • Some people can find multiple points overwhelming.	Include just one point per screen when using text graphics.

Multiple Ideas

If you are using text graphics to provide an overview of a process or introduce an idea, it may not be possible to have just one idea on the screen. If you need to include a bulleted list, keep each line to as few words as possible (Figure 8-12). Then, expand on the information in subsequent text graphics.

Figure 8-12. Multiple Ideas Expanded in Subsequent Frames

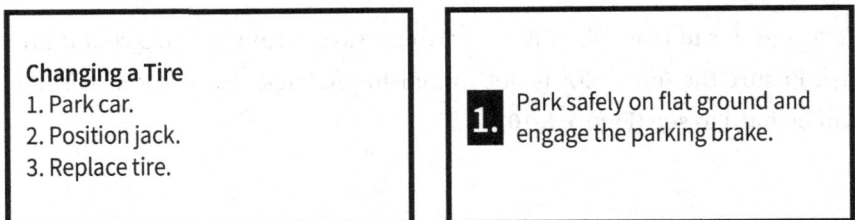

Changing a Tire 1. Park car. 2. Position jack. 3. Replace tire.	**1.** Park safely on flat ground and engage the parking brake.

Highlighting Elements of an Image

You can show a still graphic and use text to focus people's attention to a particular part. Position the text near the relevant part so viewers don't have to work hard to find it. This is something Mayer emphasizes with his spatial contiguity principle. For example, in the left frame of Figure 8-13, it takes more work to find the mic and lens, whereas the words in the right frame draw the eye directly to the part of the camera being described.

Figure 8-13. Labeling Elements in a Shot

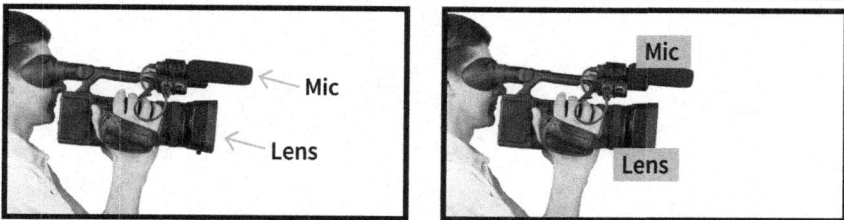

Crystalizing the Focus

If you work with existing images to create a graphic, they may include unnecessary or irrelevant information, such as a background. However, you can usually remove those elements using a program like Photoshop. Doing so allows the viewer to focus their attention on the key information without being distracted (Figure 8-14).

Figure 8-14. Remove the Background to Bring Focus

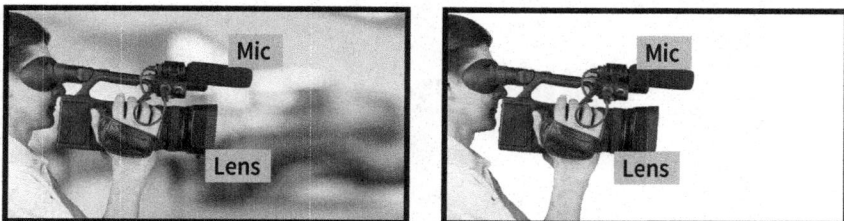

What Does All This Mean?

The process of planning pictures takes time to get used to, especially because we were trained from a young age to communicate with words. Getting used to conveying information visually, using key elements of visual grammar (such as shot sizes, camera angles, and composition), and drawing storyboards takes effort and can feel time consuming at first. But stick to it! After a while, the planning process will become intuitive, save you a lot of time and energy, and lead to much better videos.

How to Make Your E-Learning Videos More Accessible

WITH DIANE ELKINS

> **Key takeaways:**
> - Video is a powerful modality for showing physical tasks and emotions and creating vivid memories.
> - Content can easily be made accessible with the addition of simple tools like captions and audio descriptions.
> - You'll save production time if you plan for accessibility at the start of your project.

When I asked e-learning veteran Diane Elkins how the ability to film videos in-house has rocked the e-learning world over the past 10 years, she said, "We get to figure out what the best instructional approaches are, and regardless of the budget, can probably make them happen."

Co-founder of award-winning company Artisan E-Learning in Northern Virginia, Diane has been in e-learning for more than 20 years and says video today is so much easier to execute. "There are so many things you can do yourself that before you had to buy thousands of dollars' worth of equipment for.

"Video is great for showing perspective and context and giving a sense of time and space," she says, adding that she values it for showing physical tasks and emotions and creating vivid memories.

Diane's company recently crafted a series of training videos showing physical education teachers how to teach soccer to kids so they had something more than a static, two-dimensional PDF of instructions. "We filmed it in North Carolina in a gym full of sweaty kids. To create perspective, we filmed with a drone, and used a handheld on the ground."

It's a powerful example of how video can create a rich learning experience that shows the true dynamics of the game in action. The drone produced a bird's-eye shot, providing a sense of how to organize kids in space and time, while handheld cameras captured movement on the ground and emotions on the kid's faces.

Accessibility

But, as powerful as video is, does it serve everyone?

"Our job as learning designers is to help everybody learn," Diane says. "And that means everybody. We don't want to say, 'Our training can help you be better at your job, but only if you can hear,' or, 'You'll learn so much from this video, as long as you're not colorblind.'"

Countless tools exist to support video accessibility, as well as standards to guide you, but starting with the right mindset is key. "It helps to first think about people and barriers they may face while watching," she suggests. "Some may want to watch my video but can't hear it. Well, closed captions are my solution. There's no reason not to use captions."

Additionally, "some may be unable to use a mouse, so I can build interfaces where people can control video replay with a keyboard or assistive technologies. Someone may have low-contrast vision, so think about overlay text—don't put white text on a really light background."

Making video accessible starts before anyone picks up a camera; for example, being intentional with your words when writing scripts.

Diane describes a handwashing video: "I could film myself washing my hands and say, 'Wash your hands up to this point.' You could see 'this point' if watching the video; however, if someone can't see, they're left guessing. If we instead say, 'Wash up to the wrists,' it becomes clear."

When there's too much visual information to convey in the script, audio descriptions are key. Spoken descriptions of what is happening on screen can be spliced into a second version of the video so people can listen on demand. "The audio description may say, 'Diane is washing her wrists up to about 3 inches past her hand.'" Concrete language describes what is happening and makes it accessible to more people.

Making Accessibility Part of Your Workflow

Adding captions, recording audio descriptions, and preparing the video interface for use without a mouse can add time to production. But how much? And when should you do it?

"If you wait until the end, the additional time will be 50 to 70 percent extra effort," Diane says. "But start planning at the beginning and it will be closer to 20 percent." And it's 20 percent well spent.

Diane's advice is to plan for accessibility from the start. Make it part of your workflow so you don't have to go back and catch up. When you begin writing the script, be intentional with your word choices so you don't have to go back to them when you remember accessibility later.

AI can help; for example, it can automatically generate captions that you can then edit for accuracy. Online contrast checkers can help you determine if you have the right contrast between the text and background—Diane uses WebAIM's contrast checker (which you can find at webaim.org/resources/contrastchecker).

We can do just about anything with video because it no longer costs thousands of dollars, and Diane notes that the costs of making video accessible have plummeted too. With a little extra effort, you can use easily available tools to make sure that the learning videos you produce are truly for everybody. As she says, "Everybody means everybody."

Diane Elkins is the co-founder of Artisan E-Learning, a custom learning design firm; connect with Diane at linkedin.com/in/dpelkins.

PART 3
TOOLS OF THE TRADE

Masters of a craft carry well-worn toolkits that help them efficiently do their jobs. So, what tools does a trainer need to consistently plan, film, and edit high-quality instructional videos? And how should they use them to get the best results? In this part, I explore key tools you need to film and edit video using your smartphone and a nonlinear video editing software package. I also discuss some tools that you don't need but are nice to have to speed things up and because they are just fun to use. In addition, I look at how to use these tools to create polished, engaging videos that look like they've been professionally filmed and edited.

PART 3
TOOLS OF THE TRADE

Chapter 9
The Videographer's Toolkit

In this chapter, you'll learn about:
- Essential gear—smartphones, editing software, and computers
- Helpful gear—stabilization gear and external microphones
- Serious tools—lights, lenses, apps, drones, and multitools
- Miscellaneous extras—what you need in your back pocket

A friend of mine is a handyman. Whenever my wife and I have a problem in our house, he turns up in paint-stained overalls carrying an impressive bucket of tools crammed full of clamps, screwdrivers, saws, and things I've never heard of. It seems like he has a tool for every job, and I don't think he's ever been unprepared to fix something.

Tools are the stock of any profession, and for people working in TV and film, they're usually numerous and expensive. Professional TV cameras and lighting rigs cost thousands of dollars. As a learning professional, you don't need those expensive tools because you carry a production studio in your back pocket or bag—your smartphone. It's ready for action whenever you need it.

When I was based at the BBC's Elstree Studio campus in north London—where a part of the BBC's TV training department was located—I asked a colleague, who taught camera skills to staff, to name the lowest cost camera I could get away with using for filming TV-quality video. He told me that I was asking the wrong question and that it's more about "the lowest level of skill you can get away with." He also told me that good camera operators can produce top-quality video, even with consumer cameras. With that in mind, this book is about filming training videos, rather than cinematography, fast and on a budget, so I'll share some thoughts about buying new smartphones and adding other helpful tools to your toolkit. But, it's your skill and how you use the camera that is more important.

In this chapter, I identify what you need to create training videos. You can build your videography toolkit without spending much money, which frees up cash you could use for other key tools. First, I discuss essential gear. Then, I consider tools that will help you elevate your video from amateur to semiprofessional quality. Last, I list some serious tools for video geeks and folks who love gadgets, as well as toys that most people don't need but are fun to use.

Essential Gear

There are three things you absolutely need for making video: a smartphone, editing software, and an editing device (which is most likely a computer but could also be a phone or tablet).

The Smartphone

The first thing a videographer needs is a camera. However, what used to be a standalone piece of equipment is now embedded in your smartphone, which can record impressive high-definition video. It's not for me to rank the best and worst makes and models of smartphones, but I can review various features to help you decide what works best for you.

Although smartphones capture amazing quality footage, the picture quality and practical functionality are limited by the phone's small size. A traditional video camera zoom lens can physically extend, requiring space a smartphone simply doesn't have. So, smartphone camera functions like zooming and focusing are performed digitally rather than optically, which causes pixelation and blurry resolution. If the camera moves, such as to follow someone walking, the autofocus has to keep adjusting so the sharp look of a well-focused shot will come and go. Although some technologies minimize this effect, there's still some smoke and mirrors that go into great shots—and they don't always turn out well. Your smartphone camera's quirks won't make or break your video, but you should keep them in mind while shopping. I'll cover some tactical strategies for overcoming your smartphone's limitations in the next chapter.

Due to the size of a typical phone, many of the traditional controls found on a standalone camera are automatic in your phone—for example, auto focus, auto exposure, and automatic level control for audio. This automation robs you of some control. The sensors in smartphones are also smaller than traditional cameras. Larger sensors capture more light and thus better pictures. So, higher-end videographers must intimately learn the smartphone's capabilities and discover workarounds to ensure good-quality shots. However, the purpose of this book is not to create cinema quality video; it's to help you learn new skills with video as a tool. Having the best camera is not necessary—it's about skill.

So, what specifications should you look for in a smartphone?

Resolution

Resolution refers to the quality of your video as captured and displayed. At a high level, resolution technology has progressed from standard definition (SD) in the 1990s, to high definition (HD) in 2000, and to ultra-high definition (UHD)—the current standard for top quality video—in 2015.

Video frames are made up of tiny square dots called *pixels*—a combination of the words *picture* (pix) and *elements* (els). Resolution is measured as a ratio of how many pixels run across the screen (horizontally) and how many run down the screen (vertically). The more pixels in a square-inch frame, the higher the quality because the smaller pixels provide more detailed images. The SD aspect ratio is 720 x 480, which means it has 720 horizontal pixels and 480 vertical pixels. HD resolution is either 1280 x 720 or 1920 x 1080. SD and HD resolution are commonly referenced by the vertical number, which is often described as the number of lines, so SD and HD can also be referred to as 480 and 720 or 1080, respectively. To confuse things, UHD, which includes 4K and 8K frames, uses the number of horizontal pixels to describe the resolution. So, 4K resolution is 3840 x 2160, and then 3840 is rounded up to 4000.

What does this mean in practice? Most learning platforms stream video at 720 or 1080, but some still stream at 480. In the future, you can be sure they'll stream at 4K and 8K. So, when you choose a smartphone, it makes sense to buy one with a camera that has as high a resolution as possible. While that high resolution won't make an impact today, it will future proof your shots for when 4K and 8K are the standard.

Megapixels

Digital images are composed of millions of pixels. Each one has subpixels that emit the colors red, green, and blue, which screens combine to form other colors, just as an artist mixes primary colors like blue and red to create secondary ones like purple. Generally, the more pixels per square inch, the better the image's resolution—meaning it's clear, crisp, and able to show more detail. This is referred to as PPI—the number of pixels per inch. When buying a new camera, many people will often check how many megapixels a camera captures. Most smartphone cameras have at least 12 megapixels, which is the ideal; after 12 megapixels, anything larger offers a diminishing return on improved resolution.

Frames per Second (FPS)

Just like in the old days of cinema when movies were shot on film, your smartphone captures tiny micro-moments of action at a high speed. Each individual moment is captured as a single photograph or frame. FPS refers to how many single frames are captured for every second of video. The higher the frame rate or FPS, the smoother the picture and the larger the file size. American TV has just under 30 frames for every second of action. If you plan to film action, you'll want your smartphone camera to film at a rate of at least 30 FPS. If you plan to then turn it into slow motion, you'll need the capacity to film at 60 to 70 FPS so that your slowed-down video renders smoothly rather than choppily.

Sensor Size

At a very basic level, the *sensor* is the component of your smartphone that turns what you are filming into an electrical signal. This very thin piece of silicon determines how much light to let into the picture. Light is critical for filming because it affects the range of colors and dynamics between light and dark elements in your shots, as well as the sharpness. Generally, the larger the sensor, the better your picture quality because it can capture more light. Larger sensors also work better in poor lighting situations.

Because phones are small, their sensors can be a fraction the size of DSLR cameras, but new technology continues to improve them. When comparing cameras, consider their sensor sizes. As sensor specifications continue to change, research current specs when making a decision or talk to the salesperson selling you the phone.

Lenses

Lenses are another key aspect that changes constantly. Most smartphone cameras have digital zoom lenses, although this is starting to change. When possible, look for smartphones with an optical-zoom lens. Optical lenses actually move, whereas digital zoom is managed digitally. *Zooming* is a process of changing the focal distance to make a person or object appear closer or further away and is traditionally achieved by the movement of lenses and mechanical elements within a camera. Because optical zoom lenses require space to operate, they aren't common on very thin smartphones. That is changing, albeit most models with optical zoom are only offering 2x zoom.

Stabilization

A salesperson may try to sell you a phone with superior image stabilization (or the phone's ability to digitally create a shot that looks smooth and steady), but, to be honest, I've never felt good about electronic stabilization. Perhaps I'm simply being a snob, but superior stabilization in my mind comes down to how you hold the camera (which I discuss in the next chapter), more than how good the image stabilization software is.

I'm a big fan of getting the picture right the first time (which becomes second nature after practice) so you don't need software like image stabilization to rescue it. It's your call if such a feature is important, but I'd be less inclined to use it as a deciding factor when choosing a smartphone.

Editing Software

When you film a video with multiple shots, all of which are separate video files, you'll need a tool that can combine them into one final seamless product. That tool also needs the capacity to cut out the bits that you don't need and add effects that you do need. In the old days, film editors literally cut film strips and used special tape to join them together. Today, it's all done digitally using video editing software.

You'll often hear debates about which editing software is best. I'm agnostic because, like cameras, it's not the program that guarantees a good edit, but the decisions the editor makes about what to cut out, how to sequence clips, and what transitions to use. I've seen top video editors make more engaging video with the old Windows Movie Maker software than kids with souped-up versions of Apple's Final Cut Pro or Adobe Premier Pro.

When selecting editing software, choose one that best suits your workflow. A key consideration is how often you'll create video. If you're only doing it occasionally, don't get a complex software program that you have to relearn every time you log in. But if you're editing video every day, consider more high-end software so you can take advantage of its more advanced features.

Choosing Video Editing Software

Videographers can debate endlessly about the best video editing software, but most products work well. I suggest you choose the package that best suits your workflow, as well as how often you plan to use it:

▶ **Occasional users** edit one or two videos a month, or create many all at once, but then won't touch video for a few months. Because they're busy doing the other things that trainers do—like running workshops, designing learning, and coaching—they find themselves forgetting about the software. So, every time they sit down to use it, they have to learn how to use it all over again. Folks in this category will find programs like Clip Champ (Microsoft), Rush (Adobe), iMovie (Apple), and Camtasia (TechSmith) great options. These are all easy to use and quick to learn.

▶ **Regular users** spend a day or so every week making video. They don't need to learn the software every time they log in, so using it is almost like driving a car—they can perform most functions without thinking. A good starting point for regular users is Camtasia because, while it's easy to use, it also offers functions that take your videos to the next level with tools like annotations. For more focused video functionality (although, you'll lose the easy annotations), you might consider Premier Elements (Adobe), Power Director 365 (Cyber Link), or Pinnacle Studio and Vegas Pro (Magix).

▶ **Professional users** make video full time and need advanced tools like color correction, advanced manipulation, and control over audio functions like equalization (EQ) and compression. This book wasn't written for professionals or semiprofessionals, but if you aspire to reach that level, consider DaVinci (Black Magic), Premier Pro (Adobe), Final Cut Pro (Apple), Vegas Pro (Magix), and Avid (Avid Technologies). I've used Vegas Pro since it was a Sony product years ago, and although it never really took off, I have loved it.

I make these recommendations cautiously—my suggestions are not set in stone—as a general framework so you can reflect on what works for you. Always think about price and workflow to find what suits your way of working. And, consider other applications in your software ecosystem. When asked to audit training departments' media production teams and processes, I often see people using software that's way more complex than they need, which slows them down as they're constantly looking for settings, menu options, and special effects, rather than crafting effective learning content.

Editing Hardware

The next piece of gear you need is a computer with enough RAM and processing power to run video editing software. I stopped trying to remember which processor or video card is best about 10 years ago because they are updated too often. But you can easily figure out what to buy by searching the internet or asking a salesperson. As a rule of thumb, I suggest buying a gaming computer. It doesn't need to have the highest specs; the real-time processing needs of gaming are higher than video because it has to happen in real time. A basic gaming computer will have a good video card, enough RAM, and lots of hard disc drive storage space. Also, many software packages now offer editing in the cloud, which takes some pressure off processing speeds.

If you can, opt for two monitors for an expanded visual workspace. Again, recommending any specific specs will date this book very fast because technology continues to develop. Make sure you research and compare different models before spending any money.

Of course, you don't really need a computer. You can use a slimmed down version of editing software on your phone or tablet for basic video edits, such as creating microlearning videos about performing a simple task. Great apps include Adobe's Rush LumaFusion as well as iMovie and Filmmaker Pro. Some of these apps allow you to edit seamlessly between platforms. For example, you can do some rough edits on the run, and then finish them on your desktop. Mobile devices offer portability so video is edited before you get back to your desk. The downside is the small screen size compared with desktops, so editing may require extra attention to smaller details within each shot.

Helpful Gear

You can easily film great video with just a camera and editing software on your computer or mobile device, but you should use an external microphone to ensure audio sounds professional and is easier for viewers to hear. Also, to make your video look more professional with less distractions, I strongly suggest using a stabilizer.

Microphones

Although the microphones embedded in many phones are respectable, they are positioned too far from the sound source. Good audio requires the microphone to be placed within a few feet of the sound. If you're filming a mid-shot or wide shot of someone talking, the camera will be 5 to 15 feet away from the person's mouth, which means a built-in mic will pick up more of the room's ambience and less of the speaker. This exacerbates the room's echo and picks up distractions like air conditioning. The best way to solve this problem is with an external microphone that you can position within a few feet of the person's mouth. That's why you see TV presenters wearing clip-on microphones. Without an external microphone, you'll have to move your phone closer to the person speaking, leading to unnatural close-ups.

Types of Microphones

Videographers use three common types of microphones:

- **Shotgun mics** are shaped like the barrel of a shotgun. They are more sensitive to the audio in front of them than from the side, so you can pick up the sound or voice the mic is aimed at. They are often called *directional microphones,* and some musicians refer to them as *boom mics* because they're mounted on boom stands. In film production, a boom operator will mount the microphone on a long boom and hold it over the actor, just out of the camera's shot, to pick up the person speaking. In video production, shotgun mics are generally covered with a *windsock,* which is colloquially called a "dead cat cover" because it looks like a dead cat. (I've never liked this term because I like cats, but oh well.) The windsock reduces the noise of blustering wind when filming outside and can dampen some of the air conditioning noise when filming inside.
- **Lavalier (lav) or tie-clasp mics** clip onto the speaker's lavalier. Usually, the wires are concealed inside the speaker's shirt or blouse. Lav mics are great for sounds within 2 or 3 feet. So, if

you're filming inside a building, you'll hear the person's voice rather than the air conditioning, minimizing the room's ambient echo.

- **Handheld mics** are often called *reporter mics* because that's what they use for live TV reports. Often, the mics have flags attached to them to promote the TV station's brand. Reporter mics are what people are most familiar with because they see them in church halls, school assemblies, and recording studios. These mics enable the person on camera to hold the mic within 2 or 3 feet, as well as position the microphone toward another person they might be interviewing.

Which Mic Should You Use?

While videographers usually use either a shotgun or lav mic, no microphone is perfect for every situation. Think carefully about what sound you want to capture:

- ▶ **Use a shotgun mic when interviewing multiple people in the same shot.** They are versatile and can be quickly aimed toward where people are talking. However, they're heavy to hold for long periods of time.

- ▶ **Use a lav mic for interviews and talking-head videos.** They aren't as portable as shotgun mics and take longer to set up, but they're more discrete and don't require you to hold a heavy mic. They work best in sit-down interviews.

- ▶ **Use a wireless lav mic when your camera needs to be far away from the person talking or where there are tripping hazards.** They are ideal for filming people talking while in action because the mic is fastened to their clothing within a foot of the speaker's mouth, so the person can be easily heard even when moving their head.

If you only have the budget for one external mic, opt for a shotgun mic because it's the most versatile.

Polarity

There's a complex science behind how microphones are designed, including the *polarity* or *polar pattern*—which areas of a mic are more sensitive to sounds (Figure 9-1):

- **A cardioid mic** picks up noise around the front of the mic in a pattern that looks like a heart, hence the term cardioid.
- **An omnidirectional mic,** as its name suggests, easily picks up the sound of people around the mic.
- **A bidirectional mic,** sometimes called a *figure-eight pattern mic,* only picks up audio on two sides.

Figure 9-1. Microphone Polarity

| Cardioid | Omnidirectional | Bidirectional |

Different occasions require different polar patterns. For example, an omnidirectional microphone is ideal when capturing a location's atmosphere. If you're focused on a particular sound or someone's voice, you should opt for a cardioid microphone because it will minimize the noise from behind and beside the microphone. (A shotgun mic has what's called a *hyper-cardioid pick-up pattern* because the cardioid shape is narrow and favors the noise in front of it.) Additionally, if you're capturing audio of an interview with a lav mic that is positioned within a foot of the speaker's mouth, an omnidirectional lav mic will be ideal to accommodate their head movement.

Special Features

Some filming situations require wireless microphones. Wireless mics are integral to professional TV production, and you've likely seen them on DIY and reality TV shows. They resemble a box the size of a deck of playing cards and are clipped onto a person's back pocket or hidden down the back of their shirt. This little box has a cable running to a lav mic that is clipped to an article of clothing close to the person's mouth, which transmits the signal to a radio receiver that is plugged into the camera. Professionals usually opt for ultra-high frequency (UHF) wireless mics, rather than very-high frequency (VHF), because they offer clearer audio with shorter antennae.

Recently, low-cost microphones designed to specifically work with smartphones have hit the market. Rodes, a highly regarded Australian brand, offers the Rodes Compact Wireless system. There are also options from Ulanzi, Movo, and Saramonic (the brand I personally use). When buying an external microphone for your smartphone, whether it's wired or wireless, make sure to order a model with the correct connector. Most mics these days use a USB-C connector; however, older phones use a phono jack. Double check your phone's specs so you get a mic with the right plug. If your phone has a phone input, make sure your mic has the right phono plug—mics for phone jacks generally have three rings as opposed to jacks for traditional video cameras with two or one. Also, be sure the mic works with your phone's operating software.

Camera Stabilizer

Whenever you film, make sure you have a tripod or monopod to stabilize your shots to ensure they look professional. Video footage that isn't stable—often referred to as "shaky cam" or "queasy cam"—is distracting and looks unprofessional. While some video is intentionally filmed using the handheld technique, it's usually expressionistic video art, not instructional content intended to help people build skills. I've heard some folks suggest that shaky cam conveys a creative edge, but in training videos, you want an instructional edge rather than a creative one. Therefore, stabilizing shots is important. There are many ways to do so—a tripod (which has three legs) or a monopod (with just one leg) are the traditional tools professional videographers use.

If you're buying a tripod, aim for one with a fluid head and spirit level (or spirit bubble). The head is the unit at the top of the tripod that the camera sits on. It generally has a detachable plate—called the *quick-release plate*—where the camera screws in (Figure 9-2).

Figure 9-2. Tripod Fluid Head

The head has a handle that videographers can move to pan the camera (pivot left or right) or tilt (pivot up or down). Fluid heads have a chamber that contains fluid, which absorbs vibrations as the head moves, keeping the movement smooth so pans and tilts are not jerky. Fluid heads are not necessary for static photography but they're important when filming video. The spirit level ensures that the tripod's plate, and thus the camera, is level.

There are also tripods made specifically for smartphones, which you can buy online at a low price. They generally sit on a table and have a clamp that holds phone. However, they are not ideal if your script requires you to pan, tilt, or move the camera.

If you often film on location, you'll know that tripods, especially the quality ones, weigh a lot and are a pain in the neck to carry around. Backpack journalists often opt for monopods, rather than tripods, because they're smaller and fold down easily into a small package. These are also easier to carry onboard an aircraft or squeeze into checked luggage. But maintaining steadiness with a monopod requires balance and physical control, and movements like panning or tilting require more coordination. (With a standard tripod, panning is simply a matter of moving the head left or right.)

If you're using a traditional tripod, as opposed to one designed for a smartphone, you'll need a phone rig to attach the smartphone to your tripod (Figure 9-3). They can be found easily online. Good rigs will provide something that clamps the phone into place and provides grips on either side of the phone for filming handheld (if you absolutely must). The rig should also have a quarter-inch socket for attaching the tripod's quick-release plate as well as grooves at the top—called *cold shoes*—that you can slide a shotgun mic or rechargeable lights into.

Figure 9-3. Example Phone Rig for Tripod Mounting

If you are filming moving shots—like dolly shots that involve phys-ically moving the camera toward or away from the action—you may benefit from a stabilizing device that is not fixed. Gimbals are handheld devices that you mount your smartphone or camera into to stabilize an image when filming movement. For example, if you are filming some-one walking along a street, and you want the camera to move with them, the camera will sway as you walk if you're simply holding the camera. The gimbal counteracts that sway and smooths out any bumps, ensur-ing the camera moves are smooth. Some gimbals are designed specifi-cally for smartphones and are either motorized or manually controlled with weights. Motorized gimbals need to be compatible with your phone because they have controls, such as a button for record and stop record-ing, built into the handle (Figure 9-4).

Figure 9-4. Example Gimbal Smartphone Camera Stabilizer

Not everyone has easy access to tripods and monopods. And that's OK too. When I discuss filming on your smartphone in the next chapter, I'll brainstorm some ways to stabilize the phone's camera both with and without these tools.

Serious Tools

If you decide to take your production to a higher level, you may be interested in more serious tools that can help you film in difficult situations like low-light environments, capture extreme close-ups or wide shots, and add artistic elements to create more visually interesting content. Professional tools include lights, lenses, and apps. This book isn't focused on video production at that level, but in case you're interested, here are some tools to consider.

Lighting

In most situations, you can capture reasonable footage without needing to invest in lighting. However, if you want your shots to look better, lights will add a greater dynamic range between light and dark, more nuanced color balance, and, in many cases, make your shots look crisper. In addition, you can illuminate annoying shadows, add shadows, or highlight particular elements with more light.

Video lighting is referred to as *continuous lighting* because, unlike lights in photography that flash when the camera's shutter opens, video requires constant light. Lighting can be mounted on your camera or separately on lighting stands. Camera-mounted lights work well for objects and people close to the camera. However, if you're filming from more than 5 feet away, you'll find standalone lights work best.

It's likely that your smartphone already comes with a light you can activate within the phone's menu as a flash or continuous light. You can also purchase many small light units to clip onto objects near your phone or place on a tripod or stand. If you have a camera rig (like the Ulanzi or Neewer rigs I mentioned earlier), it should have a *cold shoe*—a receptacle for sliding lights or microphones into (Figure 9-5). You'll also see *hot shoes* in camera descriptions, which are receptacles that supply power. A hot shoe can power a light or condenser microphone.

Figure 9-5. Example Cold Shoe Where a Light or Mic Can Be Inserted

Standalone lights often come in kits, although they can be bought separately. They are mounted onto stands and positioned strategically around the filming location. Today, most lights are LED, which is terrific because, until 10 years ago, they were incandescent light bulbs and got very hot, creating a burn hazard. At the BBC, you had to be certified to use lights in production because of the risk of burns, electrocution (especially in Britain where standard voltage is 230 to 240V), and tripping (if cables were not properly secured).

Lighting directors are concerned with two types of lighting: soft and hard. *Soft light* is sometimes called a *fill light* because it wraps light around an object or subject and fills in shadows. A typical fluorescent light does this. Soft lighting is generally best for instructional videos because you're less interested in special effects. A *hard light* is one that is focused on an end point, much like a flashlight. It is used to highlight a particular element in the shot and takes more practice to master.

Lenses

As I discussed earlier, phone cameras have some limitations compared with standalone equipment. Many of these limitations are caused by the phone's size. For example, sensors will not be as large in a phone as they are in standalone cameras. And there is rarely room for optical-zoom lenses, which often take up too much space in a phone.

One way around these limitations is to buy add-on lenses that clip onto your phone over its existing lens or are built into special rigs that you clip your phone into (Figure 9-6).

Figure 9-6. Clip-On Lens

Add-on lenses allow you to turn your phone's existing lens into wider angles and macros, as well as offer optical zoom. For example, if you're filming something up close, such as inserting a solid-state drive (SSD) memory card into a computer, you might want to use a macro lens because a traditional one will struggle to capture a clear shot up close or perhaps you're filming in a very small space. You may want a wider lens.

In principle, using an add-on lens for these circumstances is a great idea. However, many lenses in today's smartphones are already very good for most purposes, and, often, the kind of video you are producing for learners won't need fancy lens work. In addition, the plethora of add-on lenses under $100, many of which are made of plastic rather than glass, are low quality. If you decide to buy a clip-on lens, spend real money on it and do your research on its quality.

Teleprompter

TV newsreaders look so calm and professional and are rarely caught uttering filler words like umm or ahh because they are actually reading a script that is displayed in front of them on a teleprompter—a piece of mirrored glass that sits in front of a camera's lens. Below the glass, a screen—such as a tablet or computer monitor—displays the script in reverse type (Figure 9-7).

Figure 9-7. Teleprompter

The glass picks up the reflection, and, because it is a mirror, the reverse type on the screen appears correctly on the mirror. The camera lens sees through the mirror without picking up the reflection, and the reader can read the script as if they're looking directly at the viewer because it is reflected directly in front of the camera's lens. (Remember, the camera's lens is the viewer's eyes.)

Teleprompters are great for many situations but can also be intimidating for some folks, especially SMEs who are not used to reading expressively from scrolling text. So, be judicious in how you use them.

High-end teleprompters come with screens that bolt below the mirror and can cost upward of $1,000. Fortunately, you can also buy cheaper units that are designed specifically for smartphones and only include the mounting and mirror for between $50 and $400. You'll also need to provide a screen to project the script, but another phone or tablet will easily work. There are many teleprompter apps that will scroll the script at your preferred speed.

In my experience, teleprompter apps and cheap teleprompters are clunky to use, so don't be surprised if they cause a little frustration. While they are valuable for helping a presenter appear polished, I have yet to find an app that is foolproof. Nothing beats a TV studio where an operator scrolls the script for the presenter at a pace that follows their reading rhythm.

Apps

Most professional videographers I know don't like auto functions, and this aversion was drilled into me by my BBC colleagues. Take autofocus— how does the camera know who or what to focus on? It has to guess. Or auto exposure—what does your camera know about the mood you hope to achieve for your shot? It's a guess. What's more, if you move your phone, you'll find that the focus and exposure change mid shot, which looks very unnatural.

Video camera apps offer more control over shots than just putting your finger on the part of the screen that you would like to see in focus. Apps like Open Camera, Pro Shot, Mavis, and MoviePro give you control over complex functions—such as iris tracking, shutter speed, focus, and white balance—which, while out of the scope of this book, are things the pros like to control. Some apps are more complex than others, but some are designed for novices. If you plan to film video with a cinematic feel on your smartphone, a video recording app may help.

Drones and Point-of-View Cameras

You can happily splash out $500 to $1,000 for a drone to film as if you had hired a helicopter. At first, you might think a drone is an indulgent toy. However, a trainer who teaches people crane safety can use a drone to film a crane system's components 70 feet in the air without needing to climb a ladder or leave the ground.

Drones aren't easy to operate. For example, you need to keep your eye on the viewfinder to see what the drone is filming. I personally find this difficult because every time I look up in the air at the drone, I end up shifting its direction, which then mucks up my shot. Getting used to the drone's speed and motion requires some practice, but they offer real opportunities to take production to the next level. In recent years, laws have been introduced restricting how high you can fly a drone and the distance it needs to remain from airports. I'm not a lawyer, so you need to check your local laws. Also, if you are operating a drone for commercial purposes, as opposed to flying one as a hobby, make sure you have a license.

Another tool that may help you get interesting footage is a *point-of-view (POV) camera*—like a GoPro—which can capture action through the eye of the subject. These cameras are used a lot by sports enthusiasts, who bolt the camera to their helmet as they ski or ride a bike. This kind of camera position can be powerful.

Miscellaneous Stuff

I've been talking about all the fun stuff you can buy to take your video work to a more professional level. But I can't end this chapter without mentioning some other helpful things that you should always have in your back pocket:

- **Battery backup.** If your phone's battery dies, you'll need a backup. Don't forget to carry an additional power cable to charge your phone, including one that plugs into your car, and a power brick with a full charge.
- **Laptop.** Keep your notes and script in easy reach. Whenever you can transfer video files from your phone to your laptop or cloud storage, do it. While you're at it, delete any footage you don't need. These tasks are quicker and easier on a laptop than your phone.
- **First aid kit.** It's easy to cut yourself or have a minor accident when you're filming. Make sure you have some bandages with you, along with other standard first aid supplies and medications.

- **Painter's tape.** Whether you need to attach something to the wall or hold a cable in place, tape that you can also easily peel off is very handy to have.
- **Clamps and clips.** Often, you'll need to hold back something heavy, like a set of curtains, to let in light. Carry clips and clamps for this. Big binder clips work fine.
- **Lens wipe.** You need to be able to clean your lenses when they are smudged.
- **Camera bag.** Get a good waterproof bag to carry your kit around in. If you don't want to shell out on a fancy Pelican case like the pros use, check out budget retailers for cheaper options.
- **Tools.** Pliers, scissors, zip ties, tape measures, screwdrivers, and a multipurpose tool will all come in handy. If you have them in your toolkit, you won't need to run out for them when you don't have time. Add a black permanent markert, flashlight, notepad, and pen to be extra prepared.
- **Moving blanket.** Yes, this seems weird. However, if you're in an SUV or stacking equipment in part of your car that's even partially visible, throwing a blanket over it keeps your gear out of view.

What Does All This Mean?

Like any professional, you need a toolkit of resources to do your work. When you're making a video, it starts with your smartphone, which houses the camera you use to film. You can then add other devices—like tripods, gimbals, lights, and microphones—to get your footage just right, but don't stop there. Your toolkit should be filled with other odds and ends that you'll need from time to time, such as a first aid kit and other tools like pliers, scissors, and lens wipes. Simply having the tools is not enough. You need to know how to use them, so that's the focus of the next chapter.

Chapter 10
Filming With Your Smartphone

In this chapter, you'll learn about:
- The camera's role
- Three steps for good shots
- Good filming habits

A few years ago, I ran into some friends at a conference who were discussing their new smartphones. They were interested in different lenses to pair with their devices and some apps that would make their videos look like they were filmed on a movie camera. Cameras and their functions are a common conversation among major and minor geeks alike, who get excited by technological innovation. Whether the innovation is a phone's camera, standalone consumer units, or expensive kits used by TV producers, it's easy to be distracted and think the camera is about technology when it's really about the viewer.

That may sound strange, so let me explain. Video communication is about helping the viewer see the world how the videographer wants them to see it. So, rather than being just a device, the camera represents the viewer—the lens is their eyes. Where you position the camera is where you position the viewer. In film, if the director wants the viewer to experience the fear of flying, they'll position the camera in the front of a fighter jet's cockpit to capture the gritty act of flying fast. If they want the viewer to understand a character's nightmare, they'll position the camera to show enough elements to create fear but selectively not enough to show the whole picture. They'll also use set lights to illuminate key parts of the frame and cast shadows over others.

Of course, instructional video is less about fancy effects and more about how to help people perform tasks. To craft the best training videos, think of your camera as the learner. Just as a learner in a classroom might lean in to see how a task is performed during a demonstration, the camera should move in closer to a demonstration when you're filming it. For example, if I'm demonstrating how to change the receipt roll in an automatic checkout machine, the supermarket staff might lean in closer when I open the flap and pull the empty roll out. To film the demo, I need to bring the camera in closer so the viewer can see into the compartment where the receipt roll is. Knowing when to come in closer and when to use a wide shot is about asking, "What does the learner need to see to perform this task?"

But that's not all. You also need to consider how to make the action clear. Bringing the camera in closer to the receipt roll is certainly a good idea because the viewer would instinctively lean in if they were watching the demo in person. But when you peer into the receipt roll compartment, it's likely to be dark or have shadows that will make it hard to see. The human eye can sometimes adjust to these lighting variations, but the camera can't and this is exacerbated by a smartphone camera's smaller sensors. So, you need to get extra light into the dark compartment; otherwise, the image will either be dark or grainy.

Some folks film training videos by simply aiming their camera, hitting record, and hoping for the best. Often, that works, even if it doesn't deliver high-quality video. Nevertheless, to film training videos that look professional and are easy to watch, you need to be intentional with every shot—from planning it to lighting it and filming it. In this chapter, I explore three steps you should take to set up each shot when filming on your smartphone.

Later, I also explore some additional things about your filming location and steps you can take to make editing easier. Before I get started, I need to share one piece of advice: Don't be seduced by toys and technology. Cameras have so many fancy functions that can distract you from your primary purpose when making instructional videos. Often, the complexity of these functions slows down filming and can create confusion. I always recommend using the simplest technology with the fewest features and following some simple steps that lead to good shots.

Set the Shot

There are three steps you should follow to set up your shots so that your footage is clear, easy to see, and appears professional:

- Light the shot.
- Stabilize the shot.
- Frame the shot.

If you perform these steps every time you film something, your shots will look great and be easy to edit. They might seem over-the-top when you first try them, but once you get into the habit, filming will happen so quickly that you won't notice them.

Light the Shot

As I discussed in chapter 9, smartphone cameras have smaller sensors than regular video cameras, so they struggle to capture a lot of detail in low-light situations. Even professional cameras can struggle in low light, which is why TV studios have such bright lights. The more light shining on a person or object being filmed, the better your picture; it's as simple as that. Well-lit shots are less grainy, more dynamic, and sharper. I also discussed soft light, which wraps around the room like a fluorescent light, and hard light, which is focused like flashlight. Another important concept in lighting is the key light.

Identify the Key Light

The *key light* is the single strongest source of available light. The first step when setting up a shot is to identify the key light and make sure it is shining on the person or object. When you're filming outside, the key light will be the sun because it is the brightest source of light. However, it might be a fluorescent light bulb or a series of overhead lights if you're indoors. Indoor lighting is tricky because it's harder to identify which light source is the key light.

If the key light is shining on a person's back, it will also be shining toward the camera, so you'll want to turn everything around so that the light is shining on their face. Sometimes, you'll need to rearrange furniture. Folks in my workshops often ask, "What should be the best lit part of the shot?" My immediate answer is a person's eyes because it is human instinct to look into someone's eyes. However, you also need to think about what the learner needs to see to be able to perform the task. Sometimes, it may be a set of hands performing a task. Make sure there is plenty of light on what you decide the learner needs to see.

Anywhere you have a lot of light, you'll also find shadows. Check carefully to ensure no shadows are cast over a person's face or on areas of the shot that the viewer needs to see. When filming indoors, overhead lights often cast shadows over a person's eye sockets, under their nose, under their chin, and even in their mouth if they have slightly larger lips and set back teeth. To avoid those shadows, TV news studios often mount LED lights in the news desk or add a chin light—a light aimed up at the presenter from the floor—to pull their chin, nose, mouth, and eyes out of the shadows. Before filming, pay attention to shadows; they're easy to miss. A common mistake is when videographers forget that their own shadow is cast across the ground of the picture. Avoid this by standing slightly to the side.

Use Additional Light Sources

If you're filming an object, like the receipt roll in the automatic checkout machine, you may need additional lights. You can use your phone's built-in flashlight, although, this will quickly drain the phone's battery if you're capturing a lot of footage. Instead, consider using inexpensive selfie lights that clip onto your camera or slip into the cold shoe of your camera rig.

If you need to light a large room and are using continuous lighting that sits on a stand, you can probably use several lights. An effective way to light the space is follow three-point lighting—one light is aimed at the person or object from the front (the key light), another is aimed from the side (the fill light, which is usually soft lighting), and a third is propped up high and aimed downward. The high light will make the outline of the person or object stand out from the background. In some situations, you may even add a fourth light to illuminate the background. Three-point lighting is beyond the scope of this book, but you can find plenty of resources online if you want to learn more about it.

Avoid These Light Snafus

I've already discussed how shadows can lower the quality of your video, especially those cast by the videographer across the frame. And I've discussed how poor lighting can obscure what the viewer needs to see or make the image grainy. Another common challenge is filming into light, which creates a silhouette effect. This happens when someone stands in front of a light source, like a window or external door, and the light coming through it is so bright that they look like a shadow. In some circumstances, it's not a problem; for example, the light is brighter inside than outside at certain times of day. You can also add extra lights to light the person or object, but doing so can cause other issues, such as throwing reflections on the glass. The best approach is to practice checking that light is always shining on the object.

Stabilize the Shot

Video footage looks more professional when it is steady. It's OK for the frame to occasionally have some minor movement, but this should be the exception rather than the norm. The most effective way to minimize movement is by stabilizing the camera on a tripod or monopod. If you're filming a moving shot that requires you to move your camera, such as following someone as they walk down a corridor, you can create a steady flow by clipping your phone into a camera rig or gimbal.

Using a Traditional Tripod

Traditional camera tripods come with a spirit level (or spirit bubble) to help you adjust the length of the legs to compensate for sloping ground. The release plate—which attaches to your camera rig—on top of the tripod should be perfectly level, and the tripod's legs should be fully spread so it doesn't topple over (Figure 10-1). Many tripods have straps between the three legs to ensure they're fully spread.

Figure 10-1. Smartphone Mounted on a Tripod for Stability

Using a tripod means that you don't need to hold the camera steady, which is nearly impossible because it's tiring. Tripods also take a lot of pressure off you so you can step back to view the screen. Don't forget that if you are using a traditional tripod, you will also need a phone rig—a device that holds your phone and screws into the quick-release plate.

Using a Lightweight Phone Tripod

If you're filming in an office, you may not need a traditional tripod; instead, you can opt for a desktop system designed specifically for smartphones that is small and easy to carry around. Often, they incorporate a selfie stick, which extends the phone so you can get more interesting angles. There are more models than I have space for here, so it's worth just typing "phone tripod" into an online retailer's website and choosing something you like. You'll find that some offer remote control buttons on the stand itself while others are manual. At the end of the day, it does not matter what tripod you choose, as long as you get one to steady your shots.

Using a Monopod

If you don't use a tripod, you can opt for a monopod. Folks who want more than a lightweight phone tripod but don't like carrying around a traditional tripod might prefer a monopod because it is light and easily folds up, making it convenient for travel. They have other benefits too. For example, you can hold a monopod high to get high-angle shots because it's lighter than a traditional tripod. They're also usually cheaper to purchase. And if you need to move the camera during a shot while remaining steady, it doesn't limit you like a tripod. Monopods are especially helpful when you are filming lots of short shots and need to move around quickly.

However, it can take a while to get used to using a monopod. The key is to ensure it is firmly on the ground so it acts as a stabilizer. Some monopods come with a kickstand you can rest your foot on, which makes leaning in and out easier and steadier (Figure 10-2).

Figure 10-2. Monopod With a Kickstand

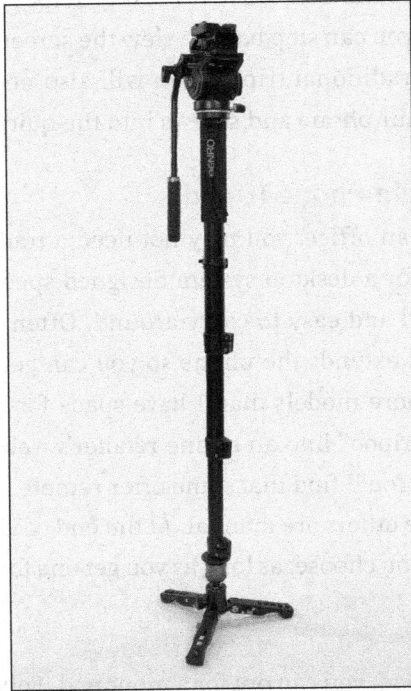

There are many other ways to stabilize a monopod if you don't have a kickstand. For example, you can stand so your two legs act as the other two legs of a tripod. Or, you could lean it against one of your feet for stability, although that means the monopod will be at an angle (Figure 10-3).

Figure 10-3. Monopod Under Foot

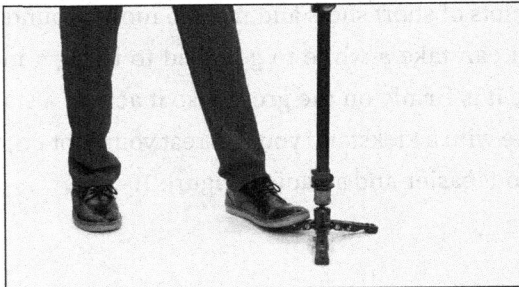

Using a Gimbal

If you're filming a moving shot—perhaps following someone around a factory floor— it can be tough to capture a smooth, flowing shot because the camera is likely to jump with every step you take. But you can avoid this with a gimbal. Remember, gimbals can be manual or motorized and have a system of weights and motors that allow the shot to remain steady as you move.

Admittedly, I'm not a fan of using gimbals, but that's more the result of a philosophical stance and the legacy of what I was taught at the BBC. However, there are times when gimbals can help you with an important narrative purpose because they make it easy to opt for camera movement rather than movement within the shot. For instance, you might want to film a series of POV shots, such as walking down a long dark corridor or following a journey or path in an onboarding video to show viewers where to find key locations on a campus.

There are a few things to remember when using a gimbal. First, it will reduce some shaky camera movements but not all. So, if you're walking while filming, do so slowly and deliberately and avoid any abrupt movements. Second, gimbals need batteries. If you're filming for a whole day, make sure you have extra batteries. Third, be safe. It helps to work with a partner, especially if filming and walking backwards, which presents a tripping risk because your focus will be on the screen.

In addition, gimbals are typically camera-type specific. My focus in this book is filming on your smartphone, so make sure you buy one that's designed for your phone and not another camera.

Steady Shots Without Tools

It's not always possible to have a tripod, monopod, or gimbal handy. Perhaps there's an unexpected event with an opportunity for valuable footage. Maybe someone just forgot to tell you they needed video footage. How do you film without a stabilizing device?

Look for a stable object you can rest your phone on, like a chair (Figure 10-4). If you are holding the camera, use both hands. While this doesn't eliminate movement, it will greatly reduce it. You can also lean against a wall or a bookcase to help keep your body steady.

Figure 10-4. Steady Shots With a Chair

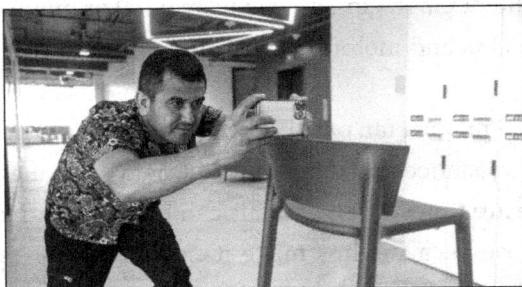

If you need to stand, tuck your arms in close to your body with your elbows against your side, which keeps your camera rigidly supported. It's difficult to hold the phone steady if your arms are extended outward. If you need to move the camera, don't move your whole body; instead, pivot your wrist, which reduces jerkiness (Figure 10-5).

Figure 10-5. Steady Shots With Your Body

One of the reasons smartphone cameras are difficult to hold steady is that they are so light. If you have a tote bag, fill it with something heavy, strap it around your arms, and use the weight to hold you down. This will lead you to apply upward pressure, and the tension between the two forces will keep your arms steadier (Figure 10-6).

Figure 10-6. Steady Shots With a Tote Bag

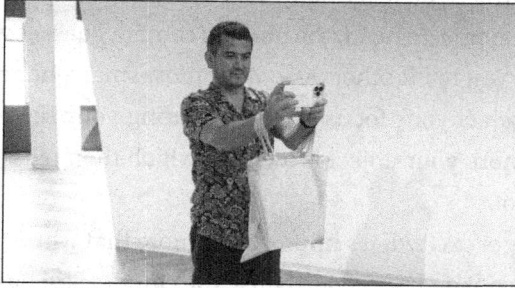

Frame the Shot

Once you're sure the person or object you're filming is bathed in plenty of light and your camera is stable, it's time to frame the shot. This is when you set the shot size and camera angle and ensure it follows the rule of thirds and is in focus. With practice, you'll learn to do this instinctively, freeing you mind to be creative with how the shot looks.

Avoid Digital Zoom

As I discussed in chapter 9, smartphones generally don't offer good zoom functions, so avoid using that feature. Unlike a regular video camera, which uses an optical-zoom lens, phone cameras simply crop the image and enlarge it. You've likely seen what happens when you blow up a low-resolution photo—it's blurry and pixelated. Digital zoom also doesn't affect the depth of field like an optical-zoom lens. For example, when you zoom in on an object or subject with a traditional lens, the depth of field changes, and the background can become blurry, which is a great effect. So, don't use digital zoom. Instead, always zoom out to the widest position, and film like that. If you need a mid-shot or close-up, physically move the camera toward the person or object to avoid cropped shots with big nasty pixels.

Some smartphone cameras are being given optical zoom functions, but they are still very limited, such as 2x. This is an improvement, but because most folks have an average camera, setting it to the wide position and moving the camera will produce the best close-ups.

Focus

Next, you need to set the focus. Smartphones don't offer manual focus like regular video cameras. Instead, the phone's camera guesses what you want in focus, unless you tell it otherwise. With most smartphone camera software, you can select your focus point by putting your finger on the part of the screen where your object is located, which then tells the camera to sharpen that spot.

Before you get excited, it's important to note that while this is likely to create focus, it's not guaranteed because the camera still has to guess. But this action does tell the camera to keep this object in focus if you move. If you leave the camera on autofocus, it will adjust as you move, which can result in some momentary blurring.

Autofocus isn't horrible; it's just not as good as manual focus, and it can be distracting. Now, if you're serious about manual functions and want to go beyond just putting your finger on the screen, a camera app—like Protake or the cheap and easy Open Camera—will give you greater control. Nevertheless, you're still not using optical zoom, so there will be digital adjustment. Phone screens are also very small, so you can't be totally sure the shot is in focus.

Use the Rule of Thirds

As I discussed in chapter 6, frame your shots using the rule of thirds. What is the most important object or person in the shot that you need viewers to see? Can you locate it at the intersection of one of the vertical and horizontal dividing lines? Are the eyes positioned on the top line? If you don't want to guess, many smartphone cameras offer a feature that overlays the grid on your screen, so check the settings. The grid won't appear in the final video but it will allow you to easily frame important elements in your shot on the lines or at their intersections. It's a handy feature to use until you're comfortable framing shots following this rule.

Set the Audio

One of the easiest ways for your video to scream "amateur hour" is to record lousy audio. Perhaps there's a dominant echo in the room. Maybe the air conditioning is as loud as the person speaking. Or maybe the person on camera sounds distant, making it difficult to hear what they are saying. One in eight Americans over the age of 12 has a degree of hearing loss in both ears, so you need to be extra vigilant to make sure your audio is crisp and clear (Lin, Niparko, and Ferrucci 2011).

Therefore, it's important to position the microphone close—within several feet—to the person speaking or the sound you hope to capture. A lav mic is ideal because it can be clipped onto the person's shirt and will pick up clear audio while minimizing extraneous noise and other distractions.

You want to film each shot so that it feels natural for the viewer—like they're sitting in the same room as the person on camera. In a normal conversation, the person you're speaking with would never have cables attached to the outside of their shirt, conceal the lav mic cables under the speaker's shirt. If you are using a shotgun mic, position it as close as you can and aim it to the person's mouth, but keep it out of the shot. Showing cables or the boom mic can look tacky and distract the viewer. Again, this is about framing each shot so that it feels natural to the viewer.

As you set up the shot, do a quick test recording to check that the audio sounds good. If it doesn't, reposition the microphone. It helps to have a pair of headphones or earbuds handy so you can listen to the audio and ensure it is crisp without distractions. I also recommend that after filming speaking shots, you do a quick replay to confirm the audio is good. Despite good developments with external microphones built specifically for smartphones and tablets, they are still fiddly. It's not always easy to monitor the audio, so checking each time you record can pay dividends.

Good Filming Habits

You can't film good-quality smartphone footage without making sure there is plenty of light on the people or objects you're filming, and they won't look good if the video is shaky or poorly framed. Your video also won't look good if it's poorly edited (which I explore more in the next chapter). You can prevent issues if you capture your footage well, but there's more to it. You need to have good habits and be disciplined to ensure that filming goes well.

Before Filming

One of my former BBC colleagues used to tell his trainees that good camera operators are like scouts: They're always prepared. Failing to plan wastes time, so here are some good habits to build:

- **Charge your phone.** Do you have a portable power bank that you can use if your battery dies and you're away from a power source? Do you have your phone charger cord and wall adapter if you'll be located near a power outlet?
- **Confirm that your phone has enough memory to store your footage.** If you'll be filming a lot of footage, make sure you have enough space on your phone before you start. Not only should you check before filming, but you should transfer the footage from your phone to the cloud or a computer after you've finished filming.
- **Brief your team about the shot so everyone knows what's going on.** If you can brief the people you are working with about your aims before you start filming, you'll save time on location. Plus, your team will be thinking ahead already. They may also see some creative opportunities.
- **Create a schedule.** Put your schedule on paper and share it with your team and actors. Include when you will film, where you will film, who needs to be there and when, and any other issues that affect the filming.

- **Brief actors.** Make sure the actors can prepare themselves mentally for what they must do in front of the camera. Also, be sure they know what clothes to wear and any props they might need to bring.
- **Get permission.** Check with facilities management and security before you film in a public location. This includes corporate spaces, like the lobby of a building, and shops or stores.
- **Check the weather.** If it will be cold, make sure everyone is prepared with warm clothing. It seems obvious, but in TV production, lack of preparation causes accidents and illnesses. If it's going to rain, bring umbrellas and wear slip-resistant shoes.
- **Prioritize safety.** This is a big point. Do a risk assessment before filming. What can go wrong and cause harm? How likely is it to occur? What can you do to minimize the risk? What can you do if something goes wrong?

During Filming

Many amateurs film video poorly and then have to waste time fixing it during editing. For example, if it was too dark, they need to adjust the lighting. If the video was filmed out of focus, they must use special effects in the editing software to sharpen the picture. You can avoid these unnecessary tasks by getting each shot right when you film it.

Here are some steps to take during filming:
- **Call the action.** You've seen it on TV: "Lights, camera, action!" It feels a little silly doing that when you're filming on a smartphone (like a little kid dressing up in his dad's business suit), but there's real value in letting everyone know the video is recording—they'll keep quiet and know not to walk into a shot or disturb what you're filming. I'm not suggesting you follow the Hollywood lingo but call the action in some way to ensure everyone knows what's going on.
- **Roll for five.** Press record, count to five, and then call the action. This rule doesn't make sense until you start editing video. If you

begin recording when the action starts, the very beginning may be clipped off. Also, it robs the footage of breathing room in the edit. Sure, some cameras offer an "always roll" feature, but don't take a chance. This practice ensures you have no clipped footage and gives you extra breathing space for edits.

- **Check the audio.** I like to check the audio recorded after each shot. Save yourself the hassle of having to schedule a reshoot after finding out you have no audio while editing back in your office.

- **Take notes.** If you're filming a lot of shots, you'll quickly lose track of which one you have and which take is better or worse. Bring a notepad or tablet to take notes as you film. It may seem cumbersome but it saves time later. It's like all things, right? You think you can wing it, but taking the extra time to do things carefully saves you time in the long run.

- **Check with the SME that all is right.** It's always a good idea to have the SME on hand to make sure that what you are filming is performed correctly. Have them sign off before moving on because you probably won't have time to come back and film again.

After Filming

You can save a lot of time during the editing process by following two simple practices once you've finished filming:

- **Save the footage to the cloud or your computer and rename each file.** As soon as you've filmed the footage, transfer it from your smartphone and rename it. Many people think that once they have their footage, filming is done. I suggest you get into the habit of considering filming complete after you have transferred everything to the cloud or your production drive, deleted the takes you won't use, renamed the files you will keep, and saved them to where they need to be.

- **Review the footage.** If you're working with a team, you'll want to review the video footage to ensure it's accurate before you invest time editing it. For example, if you're filming procedures for equipment, a SME should review the footage to confirm the procedure was performed correctly, meeting both safety and procedural requirements. If you're filming sales videos, you may want a product manager to sign off or comment on the videos. Products like TechSmith's Video Review and Red Couch Industries' Screenlight can help with this process.

Taking care of these actions immediately after filming saves time because all the shots are still fresh in your mind.

What Does All This Mean?

Anyone can film video, but not everyone films video that is stable, clear, and engaging. Poorly filmed video often forces you to spend valuable time in the postproduction stage trying to correct the footage. As well as wasting time, it's nearly impossible to totally fix the footage—you just make it less bad. But you can be sure to make it good the first time by channeling your energy to ensure all the shots are top notch when you film them. That means having plenty of light on the person or object in shot. Stabilize the camera so there are no distracting, wobbly movements. Frame each shot intentionally regarding shot sizes, camera angles, and composition. And get into the habit of preparing the filming logistics before you head out to ensure the filming process is fast and trouble free.

How to Keep
Video Production Simple

WITH TIM SLADE

Key takeaways:
- Make sure video is the right modality for the learning topic.
- Aim for high production standards, but simple tools are also great.
- When you start, allow yourself time to grow your skills.

Tim Slade has clocked more than a decade and a half's worth of experience in learning and development, much of it focused on e-learning. A big chunk of this work has been producing learning content for video, a modality he says is ideal for teaching people content they need to see.

"My very first learning project was video," Tim says, "teaching loss prevention to retail employees. We hired actors to demonstrate what it looks like when someone is engaged in shoplifting." It's easy to describe to learners in a classroom what to look for when preventing shoplifting, but, as he explains, "The power of video is in showing people how to do what we're saying."

Tim also says that we can get the best from video by being conscious of what we show. "I script and visualize simultaneously, doing them in tandem," he says, describing writing a script and drawing a storyboard.

Fit for Purpose

Video isn't always the ideal solution. To determine whether video suits a learning need, he suggests being thoughtful about whether it is fit for purpose by asking some key questions: "How does video support the goal we're trying to accomplish? How does it work with the variables that exist with the different devices the learner might be consuming the content on?"

Video shouldn't be produced for the sake of producing video. It needs to lead to an outcome. Even if that outcome justifies using video, you still need to think about how the learner consumes the content.

Production Standards

A common concern in video production is whether to aim for high-quality production or embrace a gritty, imperfect standard.

Tim reckons he can make a case for both extremes. "I try to achieve the highest level of quality that I am capable of in terms of video quality, audio quality, lighting, editing, B-roll, and animation. But, I think the viewer wants to hear a human talking to another human."

Here, Tim touches on a recurring theme with leading videographers—whether or not it's highly polished, it needs to be authentic and human.

Video Tools—Keep It Simple

When asked about the tools he uses in his video production, Tim says that he keeps it simple. "For scripting, I use Microsoft Word. For visualizing, I use a lot of sticky notes. I will put them on a board, and it looks very similar to a storyboard—shot by shot.

"I do all my editing in Camtasia," he says. "It's a really good happy medium to use when compared with more complex tools like Adobe Premiere Pro, which is strictly for editing, or Adobe After Effects for animation."

Tim also says that he films "with my DSLR camera and sometimes my iPhone. I'm a big fan of consumer-quality, affordable lighting equipment—my first lighting set for three-point lighting was $150."

Getting Started

Everyone has to start somewhere, so what advice does Tim have for folks new to making video? "You'll need to create a lot of crappy videos before you learn to make really good ones," he says. "So, just create the videos and figure out how you'll do better next time."

Tim Slade is a speaker, author, and freelance e-learning and multimedia designer; connect with Tim at linkedin.com/in/sladetim.

Chapter 11
Editing Training Videos

┌───┐

In this chapter, you'll learn about:
- Editing principles
- Editing tools
- The editing process
- Good editing habits

└───┘

In my spare time, I build furniture. I'm not sure why the practical tasks of cutting word, hammering nails, driving screws, and dabbing glue on corners are so appealing to me, but putting together a bookcase or coffee table can keep me happily pottering around my garage for hours. Perhaps my day job as a TD professional, which is more intellectual, creates some deeply held primal need to get my hands grubby. Building a cabinet or dresser requires you to measure and cut many different pieces of wood— possibly 30 pieces—at an exact length, width, and depth. If you get one angle wrong or cut one board slightly short, all the drawers can look odd. It's also more than just wood. You need handles, runners, paint, and sandpaper. None of these elements make much sense on their own unless you have a clear vision of what the result will be.

I often wonder if there aren't parallels between woodworking and video production because it too is a process of preparing stuff and bolting it together to create a final product. Just as I must measure and cut wood into certain shapes, videographers must frame and capture footage that shows elements of an important task or process. If I measure a piece of wood incorrectly, the drawers end up wonky, just like framing a shot poorly, using the wrong lighting, or missing a key piece of action can undermine the final video. It reinforces the importance of planning each shot so they can be seamlessly bolted together, along with graphics, music, and sound. And like building that set of drawers, having a clear vision of the final product is important before you start.

In many ways, video editing is like taking all the pieces of cut wood and joining them together with glue and nails, making sure the dresser is square, stands straight, has handles fixed at the right places, and is covered with a good paint job. The video editing process is when you bolt everything together so that the message is straight, assets flow professionally, and you have a solid final product.

Now, a film student or amateur videographer might prefer a more a lofty definition of editing, but it's simply about bolting everything together and cutting out what you don't need to show people how to perform a task. Acclaimed film editor, Walter Murch—who edited *Apocalypse Now*, *Ghost*, *The Godfather II* and *III*, and *The Talented Mr. Ripley*—says as much in his book *In the Blink of an Eye*. Early in his career, he thought editing was all about color, structure, dynamics, and manipulation of time, but, after 25 years, he recognized that, in a sense, it was as much about cutting the bad parts out as any of these other things (Murch 2001).

The lesson for those of us making instructional videos is that video editing may require artful processes, but it's primarily about bolting together the pictures to ensure viewers can see how to perform a task. In this chapter, I cover editing principles, tools, and processes before wrapping up with how you can form good editing habits.

Editing Principles

Once upon a time, video was filmed on celluloid. Cinematographers would film each shot for as many takes as the director asked for, and then the film would be rushed off to be developed. (The first copies were called the "rushes.") When it came back, the parts of the film that were not needed were cut out, and all the rest were joined together; later, the soundtrack was added. Today, the rushes are video files, and the different elements of the film are assembled in video editing software, but the process largely follows the same principles. You record video as video files, and then join them together.

If editing training videos is about cutting out the bad parts while bolting together the important elements—like music, sound effects, graphics, and special effects—to create a seamless final product, how do you do it well? The practices and techniques editors use in TV and film production that are associated with the discipline of continuity editing can teach you a lot. In continuity editing, the message or story is what's important, not how accurate each individual shot is on its own.

It's easy to get tongue-tied when explaining continuity editing because it's a fiddly concept. Think of an episode of the TV show *Yellowstone*—multiple scenes might take place in the cowboy's bunking house, on John Dutton's porch, and in the horse stables. These scenes were not filmed in the order you see them on TV. All the porch scenes were filmed together, and then all the bunkhouse scenes, and finally the stables scenes. Each shot is a single file, and editors then import them into an editing program and connect them in the order of the story, rather than the order in which they were filmed. Returning to the furniture building analogy, you don't build a dresser one drawer at a time. You cut the wood for all the drawers at one time, and then you assemble them.

During editing, continuity principles are less about scenes and more about individual shots. Let's say you film me playing Beethoven's famous composition the *Moonlight Sonata* on my piano. The final product might start with a wide shot of me at the piano as I play. At the fourth or fifth bar, the camera might cut to a close-up of my foot pressing the sustain pedal. As I continue to play, the camera then cuts to a mid-shot of me so the viewer sees my fingers tickling the ivories. Then, the camera cuts to an overhead shot of the piano's hammers hitting the strings as I get to the 20th or 30th bars. You keep changing shot to keep the viewer engaged because one shot for a whole minute will get boring.

As far as the viewer is concerned, these camera changes all happen while I'm playing Beethoven. However, you might first film the close-up of my foot pressing the sustain pedal, and then film the overhead shot looking down at the hammers hitting the piano strings a couple days later when I'm actually playing a Chopin waltz. Even though these shots are not of me playing Beethoven, no one will be able to tell the difference. So, you can just add them during editing to add visual interest. You and I know that these shots are wrong and in fact out of place, but they work to make the final product feel continuous. Now, there could be a few problems; for example, I might be wearing different shoes on each day. If my shoes are clear in the wide shot and the close-up of the pedal, it creates discontinuity. But if you plan for that, no one will know. The principle of continuity is not that you get the actual shot as much as having all the shots work together to create a feeling of continuity.

This is not the place to get into the weeds of continuity editing other than to briefly discuss it and highlight four key principles that will help your training videos look more polished and professional and ensure the content stays front and center:

- Ensure your technique is invisible.
- Use the appropriate transition.
- Cut on the action.
- Use video bling sparingly.

Ensure Your Technique Is Invisible

Many of us have been subjected to poorly shot home movies. For example, while filming a child's birthday party, Uncle Seth might zoom his camera in and out incessantly, or Aunt Delia might pan left and right so many times it's disorienting. If it's not too many zooms and pans, it's shaky cam. When people see these videos, the content plays second fiddle to the technique, and they might think, "Gee, not another one of Uncle Seth's home movies. All he does is zoom in and out, and I had to get seasickness pills last time I watched one." Perhaps it's more subtle than that. Maybe Uncle

Seth adds funny captions and has them spinning on screen from nowhere in a font that not even the 1970s wants back.

For many amateur videos, the problem is that the technique—such as spinning graphics or too many zooms—overwhelms the content. It's common for technique to take center stage, overshadowing content. When people notice your technique rather than your message, you have failed at your storytelling. Simply put, your technique needs to be invisible.

Use the Appropriate Transition

Editing video is about connecting different shots and adding music, sound effects, and other narrative elements. Each shot must transition from one to the next, and there are four basic ways to do so (Bowen and Thompson 2013b):

- **Cut.** The cut is an immediate move from one shot to another. In the old days of film, the end of one shot was a literal cut, the beginning of the next was a cut, and the two were physically joined together with tape.
- **Dissolve.** The dissolve is when the first shot slowly dissolves into nothing while the next shot simultaneously brightens from nothing to full opacity, so there is always a picture on screen.
- **Wipe.** The wipe occurs when the new shot is wiped over the old shot, from left to right, right to left, top to bottom, or bottom to top.
- **Fade.** The fade is when the opacity of the shot is reduced to either all black or all white.

Most of the transitions you find in editing software will fall into one of these four categories. To follow the principle of making technique invisible, you should use the transition that is least obvious and best supports your narrative. Most documentary filmmakers stick to the simple cut. It's quick, clean, and hardly noticeable. However, on occasion, they may use the dissolve to support their narrative; for example, a fuzzy dissolve may signal the next shot is a flashback. I recommend defaulting to the simple cut.

Cut on the Action

While cuts are effective, they're not all equal. If the cut is abrupt, it draws attention to the technique. To disguise cutting between camera positions, cut on the action—a technique also called *matching the action*. For instance, if an actor walks up to a door, turns the handle, and walks into an office, the first shot might show her outside the office as she walks to the door and turns the handle. The second might be filmed from inside the office as she walks in. *Cutting on the action* means that you cut at the same point of action on both sides of the door. So, cut from the first shot as she places her hand on the door handle and starts to turn it. Pick up the next shot as she walks in at the moment you see the door handle move. There are no hard and fast rules because as long as there is action, it will mostly appear smooth. You could also cut into the second shot as the door swings open. Generally, you should cut from the first shot just as the action starts—the door handle is turned—and pick up the second shot from inside toward the end of that action—either when the handle turns and the door pushes open or when the door is almost fully open and the actor walks in (Keast 2015).

Cutting on the action applies broadly to most edits. If I enter an office corridor and walk a few feet, you could change the camera position and cut to me at the end of the corridor entering another door. There is room to imply that time has passed. This is part of continuity editing—you're telling the story of me walking down the corridor to enter the door at the end; you're not showing every second of every footstep, so it doesn't matter if you cut some of them out.

Use Video Bling Sparingly

I suspect this is the editing principle that will likely get me into trouble because I suggest you avoid doing stuff that's fun. First, I don't like green screen—it's used way more than necessary and is just a pain to work with (although, I confess, AI is making it easier). I cringe when I see fancy transitions like lens flares and blind transitions because they usually distract from the content and are unnecessary. And I shudder at fancy effects like turning footage into cartoon-like animation or adding flying text effects.

Professional editors use special effects—video bling—only when they have a narrative purpose. Amateurs use video bling to show off their software skills and because adding effects is fun. Perhaps it makes them feel like moviemakers. Be very careful if you're using spinning graphics or other fancy effects because they can distract viewers from the topic and make your technique too visible. And if you use special effects too often, they're no longer special.

Editing Tools

Video editing software—such as iMovie, Clip Champ, Premier, or Camtasia—allows you to assemble all your video files, along with music, graphics, and sound effects, in one place. It also allows you to correct poor footage by improving the color dynamics or adding effects like transitions and filters. Technically, each individual file (whether it's a graphic, video clip, voice-over, or music track) is referred to as an asset, and all the assets are assembled on a timeline and joined together seamlessly.

If you have ever done video editing, you have probably experienced the program slowing down or even freezing up. Because it is pulling many different files, video editing takes a lot of processing power, even for computers with high-end video cards. So, don't be disheartened by technical mishaps as you edit, and allow yourself plenty of time, knowing you may need to reboot your computer a few times if you're working on a particularly complex project. And save often!

As I mentioned earlier, it's not software that makes good editing, but your decisions. Where you cut, how you cut, and what you do with other assets is what makes the magic. You might call me software agnostic. If you like iMovie, use it. If you prefer Camtasia, use it. What's important is that you use it well. Just like writing a book, it doesn't matter if you write it in Google Docs or Microsoft Word. What matters is you choose the right words and put them in the right sequence.

For the purposes of this book, I am not discussing editing apps on phones and tablets because most instructional designers edit on their desktop computers.

Editing Interface

Most editing software program interfaces include four different work-spaces (Figure 11-1):

1. **Monitor**—where you see the video you are editing.
2. **Timeline track**—where you position media assets like video and audio in sequence. Most software allows multiple tracks to over-lay video, graphics, and audio.
3. **Menu**—where you access important tools like media assets, tran-sitions, and visual effects.
4. **Editing tools**—where you select tools for tasks such as trimming clips, manipulating footage, and changing opacity levels.

Figure 11-1. Example of TechSmith's Camtasia's Interface

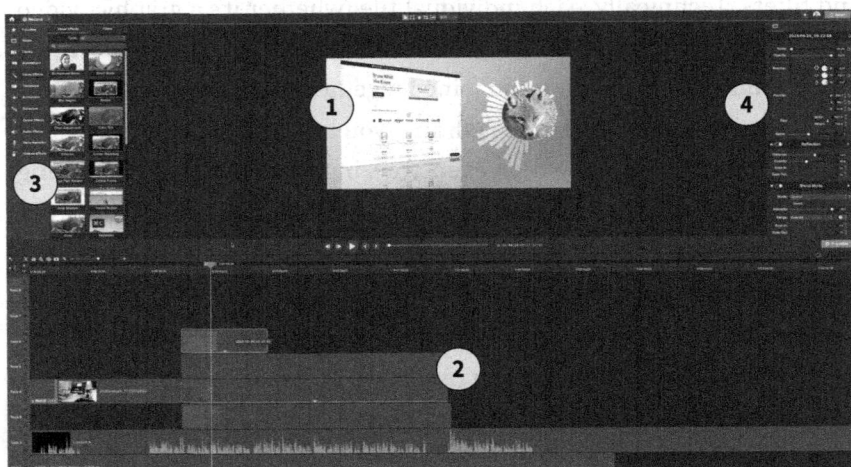

Editors import all the media assets into the editing program and store them in the media bucket. Then, they position the assets on the timeline in the story order and trim the unnecessary parts of each shot. (If you remembered to roll for five when recording each shot, you'll trim almost five seconds off the beginning and end of every one.) Finally, they fine-tune the edits so they flow, bringing the message to the forefront.

The way that editing software works can be tricky to get your head around, especially the first time. In one sense, editing software is like a media player with super-charged controls. It simply plays all the shots you have filmed and saved on your computer from the drive you have them saved into. This is why editing programs can be slow—playing all those videos takes a lot of processing power. If you have 20 different clips on the timeline, the software is playing them from the original folder they are saved in. To further complicate things, if you have clipped the first three seconds off one shot and added black-and-white effects to another, the editing software has to make those adjustments when it plays the files for you.

Now, you may think I'm getting too far in the weeds here, but there's a reason. You will generally work with two types of files when editing video, and they are very different. First, the project file is only for you—you don't share this file with the audience because it's the one you use to control every aspect of how the video renders, from the music track's volume to how one clip transitions to another. The project file can be changed as much as you like. It contains information about what clips to play in what order and any effects that you've added, but it doesn't include the actual videos—only information about where they're saved so the software can find them.

Once you have finished editing the project, you need to export it as a complete video file. This final video file—such as an MP4 or QuickTime file—is what you share with the audience and it cannot be changed. In one way, it's like exporting a Word document as a PDF file so the text can't be changed. Different software packages refer to this process as publishing, rendering, exporting, or sharing. When you export the final video file, the software gathers all your files and renders them in the correct order with the added effects as one complete file.

The project file is essentially a data file that tells your editing software where to find the assets in your project, what order they are in, and how to play them together. For example, play the clip starting three seconds in, and adjust the lighting so it's slightly brighter. The final video file is your finished product. If you're editing in the cloud, the project file is saved and the individual videos are uploaded automatically, so you have less visibility into this process.

The Editing Process

Before I ever wrote a book, I used to think of editing as a review process. If I wrote a report, I might ask a colleague to edit it, which really meant asking them to check for any mistakes. They'd read through it and check for typos, fact-check it, and make suggestions such as changing a paragraph's sentence order or modifying the heading structure. I'd publish the report, and invariably people would still find mistakes. It wasn't until I wrote my first book that I discovered that you can't do an edit in one reading.

When I write a book, it goes to my editor who does a structural edit, sometimes called a substantive edit, reviewing whether I have created a sequence or structure that is logical, makes sense, and is easy to follow. She might suggest I change a chapter's structure or the order of several chapters or remove parts of a chapter. She won't waste energy looking at spelling (although she might notice a few obvious typos) because she knows that any one of these paragraphs may end up on the cutting room floor, so why waste time? With her feedback, I scurry away and make the changes.

Once I've made my changes, I send it back for the next review. This time she checks that my information is accurate and ensures I don't say anything slanderous or copy someone else's work. This review might include checking how I spelled names or places and confirming that when I talk about an object, I'm referring to it correctly. Often, she'll know the answer because editors are good like that, but, occasionally, if it's highly technical, she'll do some research to be sure. If she has questions, she sends them to me. Then, I answer any questions, make corrections, and check my references. At this point, I send it back to her.

Now, a different editor does a line edit, which involves checking spelling, grammar, and syntax. This is when a lot of magic happens, and sentences start to take a lively flow. The line edit will be sent back to me for a quick review, and if I say yes, the changes will be approved. It's at this point that the text should be in great shape. There should be no further content changes. Everything is accurate, and the changes my editors suggest will make me a better writer. Eventually, there will be another review—a proofread—that happens when the laid-out book is sent to a third editor who hasn't seen the text. With a fresh eye, they'll pick up any mistakes that slipped through, as well as look at the book's overall layout and design for visual continuity.

Now, the point sharing this story is not to encourage you to write a book (although, if you do, more power to you.) It's to highlight the fact that editing and finalizing any editorial product requires more than one review. Don't try to do it all at once. This same lesson applies in many ways to video editing. To avoid mistakes and speed up your editing process, I suggest you follow a four-stage workflow that I call the SAFA model:

1. **Sequence.** Create a rough cut by positioning all your assets on a timeline in order. Include footage, music, graphics, and sound effects. Don't worry if there are jump cuts—just make it flow.
2. **Accuracy.** Check your content's accuracy. Are captions spelled correctly? Are the tasks on camera performed correctly? This review should be approved by the SME.
3. **Flow.** When everything is deemed accurate, it's time to go back and finesse the edits so they flow smoothly. Correct jump cuts and make sure edits are not distracting. Remove any video bling.
4. **Approve.** At this point, you may want to do one final run through, but it's time to send off the video for approval.

While I've shared this workflow with workshop participants for many years, in this book, I've updated the terms for each stage to better reflect what they are about. Let's explore them in more detail.

Step 1. Sequence

The first step is to import and assemble your assets in the editing software and position them on the timeline in the correct sequence. Start by importing the video files, and then drag them onto the timeline in the order they will appear and trim them. Every video clip will contain elements you don't need, so you can cut them. You may either split the clip and delete the part you don't need, or use the trim tool, which can shorten or lengthen the clip. Different software programs offer different options for trimming.

At this stage of the process, you are only doing rough edits—you may need to make further changes later, so there's no sense in trying to perfect things (just as there's no reason to specifically look for typos when doing a structural edit). When the video clips are in order and roughly cut to size, it's time to add graphics, music, and sound effects. If you are using captions or lower thirds, add these too. Again, don't worry about perfection. You're looking for what editors call a *rough cut* so folks can get a good idea of how the video will look and feel (Bowen and Thompson 2013b).

Step 2. Accuracy

Once you've completed the rough cut—everything flows in order and the main elements from graphics to footage to music are assembled in roughly the right places—it's time to check everything for accuracy. There is a good chance you are making this video in conjunction with a SME, and this is the step in the process when they review the accuracy of the content. Are the names or terms in the text graphics spelled correctly? Are there any elements of the footage that are misleading, inaccurate, or break a legal or regulatory practice? Is there anything in a background shot that should not be there? The SME offers feedback, which you then use to fix the problems. After that, they can sign off on the accuracy. You won't need their input for the next step—flow—because it's about style.

Step 3. Flow

You should now have a rough cut that the SME has reviewed and confirmed is accurate. It's time to polish every element of the video so it flows seamlessly and your technique becomes invisible. Remove jump cuts and ensure action is matched between shots. Review special effects to ensure they support the narrative, rather than distract from it. Confirm the music starts exactly when it's meant to and balance the levels so it isn't too loud or too soft. This is the part of video editing that's a lot of fun, and it is very satisfying to take a rough cut and fine-tune it so everything flows smoothly.

Step 4. Approve

After the flow stage, your video should be ready to go. It's structured well. It's been checked for accuracy. You've fine-tuned it so everything flows smoothly. There shouldn't be anything left to do except run through it one more time. The approval stage is all about doing a final review. Look out for anything that might be out of place. Run it by another video editor with a fresh set of eyes and ears. At this point, you should also have your SME and sponsor give a final sign off on the content.

Good Editing Habits

The best editors are master administrators who carefully manage and plan. You must manage and account for so many different assets when making videos; otherwise, you can easily become swamped. The best way to avoid becoming overwhelmed is developing good work habits, starting with saving your files. As soon as you have finished filming, transfer the footage from your smartphone onto your computer or into the cloud and rename it. You don't want to lose it.

Good housekeeping ensures editing goes smoothly, so let's discuss some editing habits that you can adopt.

Log Shots and Delete Useless Ones

After saving your shots on your computer or in the cloud and renaming them, watch them and delete any that are not usable. I'm talking about miss-takes and footage you recorded by accident. There's no reason for files you won't need to take up space.

Next, create a log of each shot while they're fresh in your memory. Write your log in a way that you understand. Identify what's in the shot and anything within it that is noteworthy. This will save you from having to trawl through your footage when you come back to it in a few weeks because it's quicker to skim your written list than watch hours of footage. There is no one way to keep notes. I generally use four columns and write the shot number (as noted in the script or storyboard), shot description, location, and any comments about the shot I may find helpful when I come back to using the footage (Table 11-1).

Table 11-1. Example Shot Log

Shot #	Description	Location	Notes
2 (Take 1)	Internal WS of Nadia driving to work in a Mini Cooper	Driving along Route 7	Mini Cooper logo on steering wheel is a bit washed out because of a shadow, but the rest of the car is well lit.
2 (Take 2)	Internal WS of Nadia driving to work in a Mini Cooper	Driving along Route 7	Mini Cooper logo on steering wheel is clear, but there's a shadow on Nadia's face.
3	External WS of an airplane landing at Dulles International Airport	Taken from car-park on Route 28 near Lindsay, VW	Lufthansa 747. As plane banks right, the tail logo reflects the sun. Shot is good before that point.
4	External high-angle WS of a Mini Cooper driving into the Dulles parking lot	Dulles short-term parking lot; shot from departure level looking down, using zoom	After car pulls up to the ticket machine, an SUV drives in and obscures the car—only use first half of shot.
5	Internal OTS of taking a parking ticket out of the machine	Dulles short-term parking lot entry; ticket machine spits out ticket	All clear

Create a Folder Strategy

When editing complex videos, you'll be working with hundreds, possibly thousands, of media assets from graphics to music to voice-over to sound effects to footage, including B-roll. It's easy to lose track of these assets, so knowing where they are can save you a lot of time. Whenever you start a new project, save all the assets you need in one place so you can easily find them. Start by creating a project folder using the project's name or an abbreviation. Then, create subfolders for each of the following assets and documents:

- **Footage.** Save all the footage you'll use for the project in this subfolder.
- **Graphics.** Save any graphics you'll use in this subfolder. Include any infographics or transparencies to overlay other video tracks.
- **Audio.** Save music, sound effects, and narration files in this subfolder.
- **Documents.** Keep documents—such as your script, storyboard, and licenses for any stock footage or audio—in this folder.
- **Project file.** Save your entire project in this subfolder.
- **Final.** This is the subfolder where your final exported files should live. You might have different versions.

When you create subfolders for different types of assets, it makes them easier to find. I've seen novice editors put all their assets in one folder (or worse, leave them on their desktop) and then waste so much time trying to find a particular JPG graphic among all the music, sound effects, and video footage files. If you need something, it's easier to know it's always stored in the same place for each project.

The larger your project, the further specialization you might have. For example, you might create additional subfolders for your subfolders:

- **Footage**
  - Master shots
  - B-roll
  - Animated video
- **Graphics**
  - Text graphics
  - Infographics
- **Audio**
  - Music
  - Sound effects
  - Voice-over (narration)

- **Documents**
  - Production notes (storyboard and shot plans)
  - Legal documents (actor releases, music licenses, and IP rights)
  - Administration (schedules and responsibility maps)

File Name Conventions

Consider adopting a set of file name conventions. It doesn't matter what convention you follow; you just need to pick one and follow it consistently. And your team should consistently follow it too. Standardized file names also become helpful if you create a stock footage library for items such as key buildings on your campus or brand logos.

There are many file name conventions you can adopt based on your needs, but here are some options:

- **Video title–shot number–take number:** brewcoffee-8-3.mov.
- **Video title–purpose:** brewcoffee-intromusic.wav.
- **Shot size–location–season–date:** ws-hq_north_entrance -summer-2023.mp4.
- **Videographer's initials–shot size–location:** jgh-ws-south -lobby.mov.

Save Often

It should go without saying that saving work regularly is important. Yes, I know many programs have autosave, but I've also seen plenty of software break that promise. If you are editing in the cloud, this is not a concern. If working on a desktop-based application, always save the file to the right location before you start editing. It's easy to start editing and then forget to save everything until afterward, but it's just good practice to always save before you start and then frequently while you're working.

Building a Stock Library

If you're regularly producing video for an organization, consider building a stock library because it will save you time when you need generic shots. For example, I was working on a video series for an asynchronous class I teach at George Washington University, and I wanted some footage that showed the university's buildings. My editor had several shots on file that he could pull from his stock library. It saved us from having to go and film them, and he used those same shots for videos he was producing for other professors, which saved them time too.

Gather a collection of stock footage of major buildings in your organization along with different entrances. Consider also having functional shots. For instance, if you work for a utility company, get shots of people working on power lines. If you work for a retail outlet, get shots of merchandize displays, customers walking in the store (you'll probably have actors), and employees performing tasks like working the cash register. The more of this stock footage you have, the less time you'll spend filming them for every project because they can work across many.

I recommend my clients plan a "stock-filming day" once a quarter. Between stock-filming days, keep an active Word document on a shared drive; whenever you or your colleagues think of common footage that would be good for your stock library, add it to the document. Then, a week before your next stock-filming day, you can sit down and plan how to film all the shots. It's also a good idea to get the same footage four times a year in different seasons. That way you don't have to use footage of the front lobby in a video published in winter that has people walking in short-sleeve shirts.

What Does All This Mean?

The editing stage of production, also known as post-production, is when you pull everything together and create a seamless final product that people will watch. Nonlinear video editing software enables you to assemble footage and other elements like music onto a timeline in the order they will appear, and then trim them so they flow smoothly. Good editing means deploying techniques (like cutting on the action) so viewers are focused on the content and avoiding flamboyant techniques (like elaborate transitions and special effects) that do not add narrative value and only distract viewers from the content. Editing is a creative process, but it's also a highly disciplined one. Follow the SAFA model and sound administrative practices for naming and storing media assets to ensure you're editing efficiently.

PART 4
WORKFLOW AND BUSINESS PROCESSES

In today's workplace, there's more pressure than ever on TD departments, which are constantly being challenged to pivot to changing organizational needs. More TD initiatives are needed, and providing training content like video must be done fast. It's not good enough to merely be able to craft training videos; it's critical they are consistently and efficiently produced at a high standard. So, how do you do that? In this part of the book, I look at workflow and business processes you should consider using to turn your TD department into a video production factory.

Chapter 12
The Rapid Video Workflow

In this chapter, you'll learn:
- The value of using a workflow for creating training videos
- The eight steps in the rapid video workflow

A critical daily ritual is performed with clockwork precision every morning in the Halls household at 5:45 a.m.—brewing coffee. After hitting snooze on the alarm a few times, I shuffle down to the kitchen where I fill the electric kettle with water through bleary eyes. No, we don't have any fancy gadgets like a Keurig machine or espresso maker in our kitchen. I grind the beans myself and brew the coffee in a cafetière (otherwise known as a French press).

The process has evolved over the years and happens almost without thinking. For example, I realized about 10 years ago, in a moment of intellectual triumph, that if I ground the beans first, it elongated the brewing process. As far as I'm concerned, the sooner I get that cup of joe, the better. Now, I fill the kettle first because it takes a few minutes to boil the water. During that time, I grind the beans, prepare the cafetière, and ready the Stevia and cream. The routine has become so slick over many years of caffeine dependence that I also have time to empty the dishwasher before the coffee is ready for sipping.

We all have routines for regular tasks. Without them, life would be much more difficult. When your routines are well-thought-out, they follow sequences that save time and ensure tasks aren't duplicated, nor require us to revisit them unnecessarily. And by following them over time, they become habitual, so you don't waste important bandwidth trying to remember the next step and can instead focus on being creative, which means better results. However, routines aren't always a good thing because some are inefficient and waste time. Also, when you're bound to the routine, as opposed to its purpose, it becomes rigid and inhibits creativity.

In the world of work, we often use the word *workflow* to describe routines. This certainly sounds more serious and businesslike for important matters beyond grinding the coffee beans. But, to be honest, when I read IBM's description of workflow as "a system for managing repetitive individual tasks that need to occur in a particular order . . . distinguished by their simplicity and repeatability," I still think of making my morning magic juice. Workflows can exist for just about anything from conducting sales to managing customer service complaints to completing projects to crafting engaging training videos.

My *rapid media workflow* is designed to help you make digital content quickly. I have a version exclusively for video—the *rapid video workflow*—that I have shared at conferences and with clients around the globe (Figure 12-1). I honed it through my experience helping trainers and instructional designers develop digital media skills, as well as training media professionals at newspapers to make the transition from paper and ink into the digital universe. It's been adopted by organizations and practitioners around the world, so it's tried and tested. In this chapter, I offer this workflow as a guide you can follow to crank out videos faster and develop production habits that free your mind to focus on the creative elements of video making.

This is not the only workflow for making video, and neither is it the best or worst. It's simply a tool that has helped many people intentionally produce better instructional videos and save time in the process. It can work whether you're using a professional camera or a smartphone camera. Generally, you should expect to spend 40 percent of your production time on the first six steps, and then 20 percent on filming and 40 percent on editing.

Figure 12-1. Rapid Video Workflow

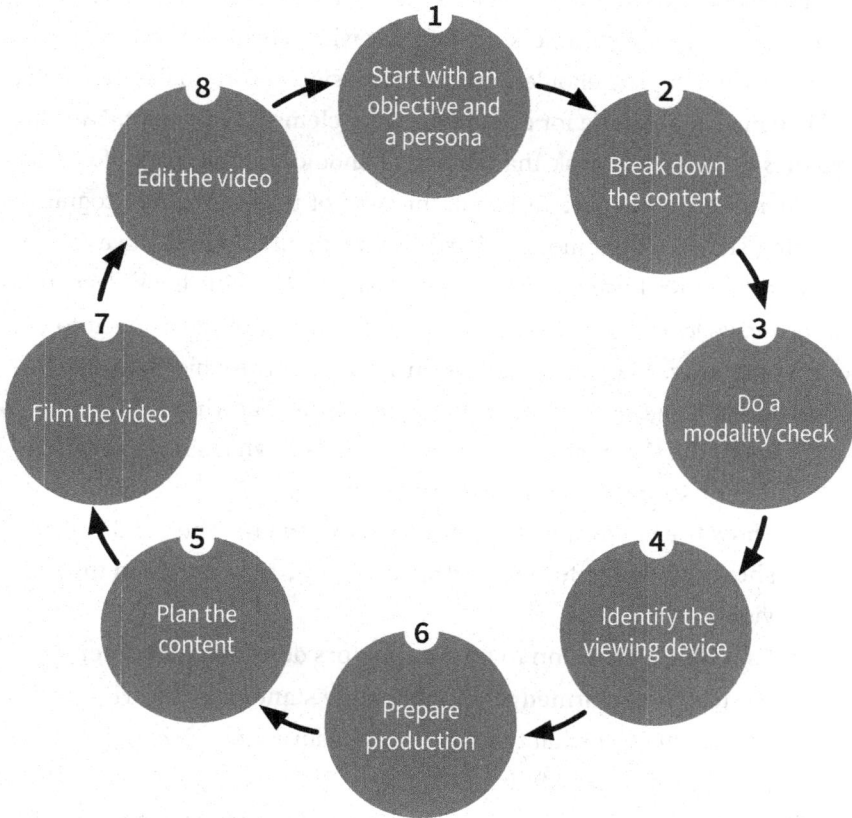

Step 1. Objective and Persona

In his terrific book, *The Filmmaker's Eye*, Gustavo Mercado says one of the most important things for a filmmaker is to have a clear vision of the story they're telling. He talks about experiences with amateur filmmakers who have lost their narrative because they copied technique rather than worked to tell their story. In other words, they liked a scene from another film and tried to replicate it even though the scene did little for the story. Instructional video is about showing tasks rather than stories, but the same principle applies—you need a clear vision of what the viewer should be able to do after watching the video.

Objective

The most effective tool to create this clear vision is the humble learning objective, which many trainers are familiar with. The *objective* is what you agree on with the stakeholders who commission you to make the video, and becomes the criteria for evaluating every element of content. *Learning objectives* describe the task that someone should be able to perform after a learning experience. Tasks fall into one of three domains: cognitive (thinking skills), psychomotor (physical movement), and affective (mindset or attitude; Krathwohl, Bloom, and Masia 1964). In his book, *Preparing Instructional Objectives*, Robert Mager says learning objectives need to describe outcomes. Mager's influence on how we write objectives is enormous, and he suggests that each one should do the following:

- **Describe the performance or task.** This is what someone will demonstrate, discuss, or show in a video.
- **Show the conditions the task is performed in.** The conditions show you where to film and specific tools that people in the video might use.
- **Establish a criterion** to help evaluators determine whether the task is performed to an acceptable standard. The criterion tells you what to examine to ensure the task is performed successfully.

The objective helps you think about what to show in the video. For example, *perform an identity check on guests* (task) *entering the parking garage* (condition) *by comparing their face to a photo ID provided by the guest* (criterion). If you don't nail down your objective before you start, you'll find yourself changing it, as well as many elements in your video, through the production process. If you're working with a team or group of SMEs, do not agree to start production until they have signed off on the objective. Then, stick to it. In my experience teaching video production to instructional designers and trainers, a lot of people question the importance of nailing down the objective until they've been through the process and see how invaluable it is. An objective helps you decide on certain scenes, music, text graphics, and narrative structure. It guides you and helps you make more incisive editorial decisions faster.

Persona

In addition to having an objective, it's critical to know who will watch your video. At a basic level, you would make a different video for a child audience than for an adult audience by being more fundamental and elementary in your explanations for children. If you don't tailor the content to the audience, much of it may be lost on them. Every person watches video through their own schemas, which are built through different training, levels of experience, cultural background, interests, and languages. Unless you are clear about who your audience is and understand their schema, you'll end up making the video for yourself.

An easy way to think about your audience is to create a persona. *Personas* are fictional characters that represent the life, interests, and behaviors of the average person watching your video. By creating this character, you can get into their heads and consider words, stories, values, or analogies that resonate with them so that you can incorporate those into your content. Marketers use personas to guide them as they brainstorm ideas and review concepts. Personas are easy to create—just think about the average person watching your video. Consider the following characteristics:

- **Age or generation** helps you understand their lifestyle, celebrities they relate to, technology they're familiar with, and attitudes that drive them.
- **Level of education** helps you choose the appropriate language level, jargon they'll understand, where to pitch a description, and how to gauge what levels of existing prior knowledge and experience they have.
- **Profession** enables you to frame the content in terms they are comfortable with. Marketing professionals may approach things with a can-do or opportunity mindset while lawyers might be more about risk management.

- **Hobbies** help you think about things that might draw their attention to the content, such as gaming, sports, and cultural activities.
- **Aspirations** can help you link your content's benefits to their common hopes.
- **Fears** help you grab their attention and frame attitudinal videos in a way that allays these fears.
- **Devices** help you make production decisions that make content work better. Identify where and how viewers will watch the video; for example, at their desk, on their smartphone, or during classroom instruction.

Draw a picture on a poster or cut a picture out of a magazine of someone you think represents these characteristics. Draw or paste images of things they like so you can get to know them. Put this on the wall to constantly remind you of who you are showing the task to. If you're interested in a template, there are lots of free persona templates online.

Step 2. Break Down the Content

When you are clear on the task that learners need to perform after watching your video, and who your learners are, it's time to get into the nitty-gritty of the content. Often, you'll create content on a topic you're not familiar with. The better you know the topic, the better your video will be because you'll be able to structure it well and find the most appropriate visuals.

So, break the objective into chunks. Instructional designers do this all the time and approach it in different ways. Some will just break it down following the Kippling method—what, where, when, why, who, and how. Others find different elements that stand out. I like to ask three questions:

- **What does the learner need to do?** Brew a cup of coffee? De-escalate a conflict situation? Set up a spreadsheet?
- **What do they need to know to do it well?** A theory? Some context? A principle?
- **What mindset should they adopt to do it well?** Customer first? Digital first? Safety first?

Each question is likely to generate multiple answers. Complex tasks could generate bucket loads of answers, whereas you could complete simple tasks on the back of a napkin. Involve SMEs for the complex tasks—consider inviting them into a conference room and put the answers on sticky notes on the wall. Move the notes around and look for patterns. It may feel cumbersome, but the better you understand the content now, the less likely you'll make a mistake that a grumpy SME identifies halfway through the project. You'll also brainstorm creative ways to show it in video.

With this knowledge, you'll be able to complete the next step.

Step 3. Modality Check

Once you know your topic, it's time to consider whether video is the best modality for instruction. On average, one final minute of video takes three to four hours to produce. That means an engaging, well-produced two-minute video will take just under a day to finish. Some people will crank it out faster, but most need a day. So, ask yourself, "Is making a video to teach this subject the most effective use of time and money?"

This is a key part of the multimodal principle that I discussed in chapter 5. You need to determine whether video is the best modality for teaching the topic and consider using a different modality if it's not, like an infographic or podcast. To decide, you can ask what I call the "classroom question": How would you teach this topic in a traditional classroom? Would you use a demonstration, story, explanation, or quick snapshot? If you'd lean toward using a demonstration, video is ideal. If you'd use a story, a podcast might be more powerful. If you'd use a detailed explanation, written text might work best. And if you'd rather show a snapshot of information or complex relationships, an infographic might be your best bet.

You won't always have the luxury to decide that video is not the best option—your boss might want a video series anyway. If you have no choice but to use video for a dense, complex topic that would be better shared with written text, you have to get creative. But whenever possible, avoid using video if another modality will be more effective.

Once you determine that video will best help people learn a task, it's time to ask the next question: What device will most people watch the video on and where?

Step 4. Identify Viewing Device

Different devices impose different viewing experiences. When you watch video in a cinema, you might move your head left to right to watch a horse gallop across the screen. You're also likely to have few distractions—the lights are dimmed, and the surround sound is all-encompassing. Watching TV can be a totally different experience—it might be on in the family room while you cook dinner and your kids do their homework. It's not an immersive experience like the cinema, so you need to think of ways to effectively keep eyeballs on your video. If you're watching a video on your phone at an airport, you likely have the sound turned off so as not to disturb others around you—you must rely on what you see, not hear.

If you know what device people are likely to watch the video on, you can film it in a way that optimizes that device's viewing experience and the conditions the video is likely to be viewed in. If you're creating video for a technician repairing equipment in a factory, you can avoid wide shots and lots of small text, which is hard to read on a small phone screen that might be heavily pixelated. You may choose not to use narration—who would hear it on a factory floor? Instead, you can use large text graphics. Or, if you know people will be watching on a projector in a traditional classroom, you can anticipate that its bulb will be old and fading, so you can increase the contrast on the final video.

If you've developed a persona, you will likely have a good idea of how the learners will watch the video. But do some more research. Ask your SMEs. Will the video be embedded in asynchronous learning or available on demand for technicians in the field? Then, determine what production considerations you need to make.

Aspect Ratio

What's in a shape? Some videos are displayed as a square while others appear as a rectangle. The term *aspect ratio* describes the vertical and horizontal dimensions of the video frame as a ratio. Film your videos in an aspect ratio that works for the device your viewers will use as well as the hosting platform you're using. The most common aspect ratios are widescreen, vertical, and square.

Aspect Ratio	Example
• **Widescreen aspect ratio**, which has parallels in print design to the landscape format, is 16:9. • It's ideal for video being viewed on a computer, tablet, or projected onto the wall in a classroom.	Widescreen 16:9
• **Vertical aspect ratio**, which has parallels in print design to the portrait format, is typically 9:16 or 4:5. • It is ideal for video being viewed on smartphones because people generally hold their phone upright.	Vertical 9:16 Vertical 4:5
• **Square aspect ratio**, which you find on Instagram and Pinterest, is 1:1. • It works fine for most devices and is preferable over widescreen for video viewed on smartphones.	Square 1:1

Step 5. Plan the Content

Up to this point, you will have gathered all the information you need about the task. You'll also know who your learners are, how they're likely to watch the video, and whether video is the best modality. Now, it's time to plan the video content. There's a lot to think about, but I will focus on the three Ss: structure, storyboard, and script.

Structure

The sequence for planning content in the rapid video workflow is very intentional. You shouldn't write the script until after drawing a storyboard, which you won't do until you've planned the structure. This surprises a lot of people, but video is a visual modality, not a spoken one. Viewers will remember more of what they see than what they hear. But, because we were taught to read, write, and speak in school, we default to our comfort zone, which is writing a script.

However, a problem arises whenever you follow a sequence or work-flow—the first decisions influence subsequent decisions. For example, if I decide to cook fish for dinner, I'll choose all the other elements of the dish based on how they work with fish. If I choose to wear jeans, I'll wear a casual shirt that I know works with the jeans rather than a formal one that works with a suit. When you write a script first, it influences every other editorial decision you make. But, if the spoken word is one of the first things people forget, then you need to start with the element of your modality that carries the power.

In this workflow, planning should start with structure, so you should always draw a storyboard before writing the script. In chapter 8, I discussed different ways to structure your content. It will be easier to stay focused on the topic at this point in the workflow if you don't worry too much about what pictures you'll choose. You can do that when you get to storyboarding. To provoke learning, always start with an overview and the reason for watching. Throughout the video, relate key elements back to the big picture, and incorporate creative repetition to support retention. There are many creative ways to do this, and you can use some of the narrative templates in chapter 8 as a guide.

Storyboard

Once you have finished your structure, translate it into pictures by creating a storyboard. I discussed storyboards and how to draw them in chapter 5, but here's a refresher: Looking at the skeleton structure of your video, go through each step and consider what pictures can show that part of the content. Load as much of the message into each shot as possible through creative use of shot sizes, camera angles, camera position, and selection of what goes into each frame. If you can't think of a picture, consider whether music, text graphics, sound effects, or spoken word content can better relay the information.

Script

Once you have a storyboard, it's finally time to write the script. It should contain a description of the pictures along with any spoken word content and other elements, such as music or sound effects. There are many ways to lay out a script, and I don't think it matters how you do it. If you're writing for Hollywood, every page represents a minute of screen time, but you don't need to do that. Many folks find a two-column format helpful—the left column describes what is on the screen, and the right column contains the spoken content, along with music and sound effects (Table 12-1). This format is more closely aligned with documentary scripts.

Table 12-1. Sample Two-Column Script

The Role of Learning Materials in the Workplace	
Objective: Discuss the role of learning materials in workplace learning. **Filming location:** Classroom B14 **Videographer:** PJ **Set:** JH sits on a desk at the front of classroom B14. He speaks to the camera with a pile of workbooks next to him. Situate a flip chart nearby in the background.	
WS: JH turns to camera	A client called a few days ago.
Cut to stock: JH talking on a smartphone while walking along street away from camera	"Jonathan, we're replacing the text in our online learning series with talking-head videos."
Cut back to WS: JH to camera	"Why?" I asked. "The boss wants to modernize our courses," she said. "Every module video?" "Yep, every one," she replied.
Cut to MCU: JH to camera	Now, I love making instructional videos. But is video the right choice for every learning topic? Especially talking-head video?
Cut to text graphic: "Learning materials are tools and content intentionally created to support learning."	Generally speaking, . . . learning materials refer to tools . . . and content . . . intentionally created to support learning outcomes. They can be printed on paper . . . or published digitally.

Table 12-1. (Cont)

Visuals	JH Speech
Cut to CU: Someone flipping through an ATD Education course participant guide	They include physical workbooks to guide participants' note taking, job aids that learners keep at their desk, and slide decks . . . trainers use to support instruction.
Cut to screen shot: Mouse on computer screen completing an interactive poll	They also include quizzes embedded in asynchronous learning experiences to boost retention, video field trips to bring the outside world into the classroom, podcast interviews with SMEs, and infographics capturing key concepts or processes.
Cut to MS: JH to camera	In some organizations, learning materials are created by learning design teams. In others, they are outsourced to instructional design companies. While in others, they are built by trainers. This course explores key issues to consider when designing learning materials. To make sense of these issues, we'll look at three types of learning materials.
Cut to text graphic with bullets: Participant materials	Materials participants use during formal learning
Reveal second text bullet: Facilitator materials	Materials facilitators use to support formal learning
Reveal third text bullet: Performance support	Tools participants take back to the workplace to support continued learning and performance.
Cut to WS: JH to camera	Increasingly, learning materials are digital. They're used in both physical and virtual classrooms. They're available in the flow of work to support learning. They're used for formal, informal, and social learning experiences.
Cut to CU: JH to camera	So, what's the purpose of learning materials? We can answer that by defining learning.
Cut to text graphic: "'Learning is the process of gaining knowledge, understanding, or skill by study, instruction, or experience.' —Talent Development Body of Knowledge"	ATD defines learning as gaining knowledge, understanding, or skills for use in the workplace. The role of learning materials is to help folks gain knowledge, understanding, or skills to do their jobs. If learning materials do that, they're effective. If they don't, they're not.

Table 12-1. (Cont)

Visuals	JH Speech
Cut to MS: JH to camera	This takes me back to my client call. Should her company be turning text content into talking-head videos just to be flashy? No. But if it better supports learning, then yes.
Cut to text graphic: "Learning materials should support learning so participants can perform their work better."	The purpose of learning materials is to help people learn how to do their job and to do it better. It's not to create flashy content. It's not because everyone else has a workbook or job aid. Simply put, learning materials exist to support learning. How can we make them more effective?
Cut to MS: JH to camera	In the next section, we'll consider three key criteria for effective learning materials for workplace learning.

When writing content that will be said aloud—such as dialogue in a role play, a monologue that someone presents to a camera, or commentary used in narration—follow media writing conventions that have evolved over decades of production. The first convention is *writing to picture*, which means not repeating with words what is clear in the picture. If your video shows someone driving a car, don't write, "This person is driving a car" in the narration because it's clear already to viewers and will just increase cognitive load. Instead, add information that is not seen but is relevant, such as "Jaya needed to meet her family at Dulles International Airport." Now, the idea of the picture is complete.

In addition to adding information to the picture, rather than repeating it, you should follow these traditional principles from TV and radio broadcasting, which are designed to make words easier to hear (Halls 2015):

- **Keep sentences short.** The longer the sentence, the longer it takes the brain to process. Consider limiting each sentence to one clause (a subject and verb). Write in the active voice and remove any words that do not support the message.
- **Choose short words.** Like long sentences, long words take more time to process and increase cognitive load. Mono syllables like *end* are more effective than longer words such as *conclude*. Avoid

abstractions that require additional words. The phrase "We will engage in a process of negotiation" is better said as "We will negotiate." Favor verbs over nouns and opt for concrete expressions like "This will increase revenue," rather than abstract expressions such as "Lead to success."

- **Write to be heard.** When you say words out loud, they can run together and sound like other words. For example, if you say, "attacks on religion," it can sound like "a tax on religion." Practice words out loud to be sure they sound clear, and, if they run into each other and sound like something else, change them so they're clear.

As you write your script, consider music, sound effects, and whether video shots need to be filmed or pulled from a stock library.

Step 6. Prepare Production

A lot of people skip steps 1 to 5 and start at step 6. Unfortunately, they end up wasting time and energy because without a plan, they have to repeatedly change prior decisions and correct mistakes that could have been avoided with a little planning. At this point, you have the storyboard and the script, and you know what you need to film and what other key assets you may need to gather. Now that it's time to plan how you'll capture them, here are some the things you need to do:

- Scout the location.
- Create a shot plan.
- Draw a responsibility map for the team.
- Get permissions.
- Do a risk assessment.
- Prepare equipment.

Scout the Location

It's not always possible, but, when you can, visit the location you plan to film to develop a visual awareness of the space, lighting, and objects that might appear in shot. If you're in a public area, like a busy building's lobby, assess pedestrian patterns ahead of time so you can plan to either divert folks away from the action or move the filming to a quieter area—you don't want people walking into your shot unless you've planned for it.

Look around to see if there's anything at the location that might be useful to you. Are there items or furniture that you can creatively include in shots or visually interesting architectural elements? Is there anything that should be taken out of the background? Because you're likely filming with a smartphone, you'll rely on natural lighting, so monitor the position of the sun, which changes throughout the day and affects the room's ambience. If you scout your location in the morning, you might plan the perfect shot with sun shining on a key area of the frame, but if you arrive to film in the afternoon, that perfect shot will be full of shadows.

Create a Shot Plan

I was running a workshop in New York City when a participant complained that I was making things more cumbersome with all my planning suggestions. "I thought you were teaching us rapid video, not how to run a Hollywood production," he said. I certainly am listing a lot of things that need to be done—you can just wing some of it, right? You can, but spending extra time in planning will save you more time in production. I once asked a BBC colleague I worked with, who had more than 30 years' experience directing and producing network TV shows, to suggest the single most important thing for TV success. I expected him to say imagination or something like that. He turned to me and said, "Jonathan, there are three things: planning, planning, and planning."

There's another good reason to engage in planning other than saving time: Your content will be better. Why? For starters, you'll think through all your shots when creating the storyboard. When you arrive on location to film, you won't have to figure out where to stand and what to show; instead, you can focus on the creative things that will make the shot look great, like helping the person in shot look natural and removing things in the frame you don't want to see. You also won't have to make up things as you go or make do with less because you weren't prepared.

A *shot plan* is simply list you create of the shots you plan to film and in what order. In the last chapter, I talked about how *Yellowstone* is not filmed in the order of the story. Rather, all the bunking room scenes are filmed together, as well as all the scenes on the porch and all the ones in the stables. They are put in order during editing. Before you film, decide which shots you will do first and make a plan. You might need to book a conference room to film all the shots you need in one. You might need to get permission from security to film in the lobby at a specific time. If you're filming a simple video on your own, you can create a shot plan on a piece of paper. When it's more complex or you have multiple people involved, you should amp up the planning and include details like location, shot number (which should correspond with the storyboard and script), what action is happening, who is filming, who is providing support, any actors, how they're dressed, any props, and any notes. Table 12-2 is a good example of a simple table that will suffice.

Table 12-2. Shot Plan Example

Time	Location	Shot	Crew	Actors	Props and Wardrobe	Extra Notes
14:15	External HQ entrance	1, 4, 7, 8	Pedro (camera) and Louis (assistant)	Philip and Maryam	Business attire; carrying cell phones	Security will hold people back for each shot.
14:45	Internal HQ lobby	2, 6, 12	Pedro (camera) and Louis (assistant)	Philip and Maryam	Business attire; carrying cell phones	Watch out for reflection off glass.
15:30	Board room 1903	5, 9, 11	Pedro (camera), Heidi (SME), and Louis (assistant)	Philip, Maryam, Sherry, Angela, and Carlos	Business attire; PowerPoint slides on TV	

Create a Responsibility Map

When you're working with multiple people, write down who does what. Consider assigning roles like camera operator, assistant (who runs around and does the thankless tasks like grabbing water bottles), SME (who ensures tasks are being performed correctly), actors, and other key players. A simple table like Table 12-3 works well.

Table 12-3. Responsibility Map Example

	Filming	Support	SME Sign-Off	Props
Pedro	X			
Louis	X	X		
Heidi			X	X
Sherry				X
Angela				X

Permissions

Whenever you film in a public place, get permission. I've lost track of how many people have told me that "It'll be fine to film there," and then end up wasting a day because they had to leave and wait for formal approval. You may be denied permission to film in a public area for many reasons. Companies that hold sensitive data or work in research and development can be especially concerned about any device that can capture private information. When I worked with a major pharmaceutical company, my client assured me that I'd be allowed to film on their campus. However, she hadn't checked and our filming was shut down. Security will throw you out if you start filming in a place like a casino because they are protecting their patrons' identities, but you'd be surprised how touchy some folks become when they see an organized shoot in progress. If it's not for security reasons, such as in government buildings, you might be denied permission for public safety reasons. The bottom line: Get permission from facilities management staff or the security office. If you want to film in a public space, like a mall or a store, check with the general manager first.

Conduct a Risk Assessment

Risk assessments are a simple but critical process in which you ask a few questions. First, what could go wrong at your filming location? It might be personal safety. Perhaps, something could delay filming. Consider what can be done to prevent those things from going wrong. Also, consider how you'll respond if they do go wrong. Safety is a risk when filming. Videographers should have their eyes glued to their film screen as they watch the shot. They shouldn't be scanning their immediate environment for pickpockets or other mischievous folks passing by. If you're walking backward while filming, is there anything that could trip you? What is the weather like? If it's cold and you're filming outside, are you dressed appropriately? If it's raining, do you have shoes that won't slip? The more complex your project, the more time you should spend brainstorming what could go wrong and creating mitigation strategies.

Prepare the Equipment

As you prepare to film, make sure to charge your phone, light, and backup batteries. Check that you have plenty of memory on your phone. If you have a wireless external microphone, charge it or have fresh batteries on standby. If you are using a tablet as a teleprompter, make sure it's charged and the scripts are loaded onto it.

Step 7. Filming

The seventh step is what most people visualize when they think of making a video. Someone stands with a camera and people act in front of it. When you've planned everything well, this step should happen very quickly. I explored filming in chapter 10, so there's no point being too repetitive. Just remember the tips I shared for filming with a smartphone so you get your shots right the first time and don't need to film them again or waste time editing to correct them with effects like brightness or contrast. Plan ahead so you don't have to go back and film more footage. Follow your shot plan and make sure each shot has plenty of light. And don't use digital zoom!

Step 8. Editing

This is the step that takes the longest. You'll likely find that editing eats up 40 percent of your production time. It's when everything comes together, and you need to pay attention to all the visual details that show the task and all the editing principles and steps that I covered in chapter 11. Remember to allow yourself enough time, adopt good administrative practices, and follow the SAFA workflow.

What Does All This Mean?

Years ago, my friends and I rented a cottage in the mountains for a weekend. One morning, I was up early making my cup of joe. (As I mentioned, I have a solid workflow that I've perfected over the years for making my morning magic juice.) One of my friends, who likes to muck in and help people whenever he can, came stumbling out of his room just after I had started the kettle. He wanted to help, but everything went wrong. He didn't grind the beans to the right fineness. He put the water in after the coffee grinds—I prefer a little water first, then the beans, and then the rest of the water. It became a clunky activity as I lost my flow, and the coffee didn't taste the way it should've. And it took longer to make.

Often, something similar happens when a team mucks in to make video together. Different people have different approaches, and, while it can start off OK, people can very quickly run in different directions. It's important that everyone on the team follows the same workflow (it doesn't matter which one). Having a workflow creates clarity. Following the same workflow extends to every aspect of production, including file name conventions and folder structures. It means consulting with all SMEs in the same way. If everyone is in the habit of doing things the same way, you'll be more efficient.

If you're working on your own, a workflow is still valuable. It helps you turn routine tasks into habits that you don't need to think about—they'll happen automatically in the right order to keep things running efficiently. And when these mundane tasks become habitual, you'll have more bandwidth to focus on the creative aspects of production.

How to Turn Around Captivating Videos Fast

WITH DANIELLE WALLACE

> **Key takeaways:**
> - Be authentic and relevant.
> - Plan your content.
> - Make content accessible.

Danielle Wallace is based in Toronto, Canada. She uses video to share information fast in a way that's practical and relevant. In fact, you may have seen her videos at ATD conferences—she regularly publishes short, 60-second summaries of conference sessions she attends for folks who can't be there in person.

What are her secrets? Be authentic. Plan your content. And make it accessible.

Be Authentic and Relevant

"Start with the end goal and provide information that's relevant," she says. Her policy is to be practical and authentic—something she draws from her marketing experience. Content doesn't have to be highly polished like you'd expect in a TV broadcast. Being gritty and real is fine as long as it's relevant.

"Marketers have been using this style of connecting with consumers for quite a while. Not only is it cheaper for production, but it allows for the authentic feeling that so many brands want."

Her conference videos aren't staged or contrived. She looks for a relevant background for context, whether inside or outside the conference venue, and then she films herself giving a summary while holding her notes and pointing her phone's camera toward herself.

"I want them to feel like they're part of the experience. So, if there's wind blowing in the background outside the ATD conference, viewers can get that organic experience."

Plan Your Content

Does being authentic and in the moment mean winging it? Danielle's videos are 60-seconds long, which is not a lot of time, so how does she keep the content focused?

"The key is planning," Danielle says, and she recommends several ways to do it: "Be concise, meaningful, and engaging. Also, think about the learner and who they are." Understanding the learner is as important as being clear about the video's purpose.

"The big central theme of a learner persona is having a deep understanding of who your audience is. That always forms the foundation for any learning piece." The better you know the learners watching the video, the easier it is to pitch it at the right level, use appropriate language, and share examples that make the most sense to them.

Planning also means thinking through how to hook the learner. "You need an effective way to draw them in, which means engaging them, so they realize 'What's in it for me?' right from the start. For example, I offer three things they can learn, even though they're not at the event."

Make Content Accessible

When talking about using captions, Danielle says, "It's essential from an accessibility standpoint for everyone to be able to read any spoken content in your videos." She adds that captions also hook potential viewers. "Captions help everyone because many people don't actually watch the videos with sound initially, so if they see the opening words, it will entice them."

She says that "there are many software packages out there with auto transcription," for both desktop computers and smartphones, but there's more to it than just letting AI software generate captions. "Captions require editing to make sure they're accurately reflecting what you want them to say." When Danielle edits captions, she checks for accuracy and uses tools to add emphasis. "I go through the transcript and deliberately highlight key concepts. No tool (yet) will do that accurately for you." She says this helps with engagement because "people who don't have the volume on can see the key highlights."

Fast and Furious

Danielle's summary videos are a great model to replicate beyond conferences. Providing summaries immediately after lunch & learns or key corporate events helps promote information sharing. Recording videos after significant learning moments increases learning in the flow of work.

A key step in quickly producing short, gritty informational videos is to let go of the need to produce a perfect video; instead, focus on being relevant and authentic—that's what connects with audiences. The more you do it, the better your videos will become.

Danielle Wallace is the chief learning strategist at Beyond the Sky: Custom Learning; connect with Danielle at linkedin.com/in/daniellewallace.

Chapter 13
Systems, Stakeholders, and Processes

Although my first paid media jobs as a teenager in the 1980s were in TV soaps, I really cut my teeth in radio. I was passionate about radio because I loved the medium and many of my family members had worked in radio during its early days. In the late 1930s, my grandfather pioneered a program for ABC (the Australian Broadcasting Corporation) that broadcasted school lessons over the radio for kids who couldn't travel to a schoolhouse. As a kid, I used to leaf through photos of the old studios and microphones he worked with. Those were the days when announcers wore neckties while they read the news—I have a picture of him doing just that. When I started working in radio, I went to classes on script writing, presentation skills, editing technique (which involved cutting and splicing quarter-inch tape), and conducting live interviews. I especially enjoyed interviewing and script writing.

The writing techniques I learned were based on conventions that were developed over decades of trial and error by radio broadcasters and others in the media. As broadcasters found that short words more easily conveyed a message than fancy, longer words with lots of syllables, they developed the rules of the trade. As advertisers discovered that long, unruly sentences littered with dependent clauses caused cognitive bottlenecks, they began to favor writing single-clause sentences that were quicker to read and easier to understand. Many conventions used in TV today evolved through practice from silent movies. I touched on some of these conventions earlier in the book because they also apply to video writing, such as constructing short sentences, using short words, having concrete language, and deploying words that are easy to hear when read out loud.

Believe it or not, we are currently in pioneering times. While we have a rich history of media production techniques to draw from, you and I are creating the future right now, just as the pioneers of the 1930s and 1940s established principles we're following today. Video has never been as important in learning as it is now. You could be creating conventions that others will follow in the future, especially dealing with how you integrate the development and production of video into your TD department's processes. I know that's the learning or TD executive's concern, but it's also worth thinking about from the practitioner's perspective.

In this chapter, I explore some ideas for integrating the practice of making training videos into the instructional design process so that cranking out a video becomes as routine for learning professionals as designing a slide deck. This process shouldn't be managed by a few enthusiasts at the office. All learning professionals should have a good grasp of how to use video and be able to incorporate it in their work. I also discuss what you can do to effectively produce video by following practices that ensure consistent quality. Additionally, I consider ways to quickly get you up to speed despite the TD profession's lack of established best practices.

The Future of Talent Development

I recently saw a cartoon depicting the traditional training department. At the end of a corridor, there was a door with a smoky yellow window and a note taped to the glass that said, "Out to lunch." There was a caption under the picture that said, "If you can't do, you teach." I'm not sure training departments in the past were anything like that, but we've certainly changed a lot. In forward-thinking organizations, the trainers are now considered talent developers, and they are a critical part of the business. The notion that training is about classrooms and programs is fading fast, and the assumption that training courses teach a topic is out of date. This thinking has been replaced by an understanding that training helps build capability and skills linked to organizational needs. To be frank, I'm excited for these changes because we have an opportunity to put talent at the heart of organizational success.

Within this context, TD professionals need to build their skills so they're available when needed. And they need to package their content to be easily accessible and structured—not just an information dump but designed to help staff develop mastery. As technology, social values, regulations, global alliances, and communities of practice continue to change, training content needs will rapidly evolve. A two-month course development project that meticulously follows each step of the ADDIE process will soon be considered a luxury for most talent development needs. Instead, you'll need to quickly produce or update content on demand. Agility is the name of the game. The role that training videos play in these changes is less clear, but organizations will need to be able to quickly produce high-quality training videos that feed into the broader learning ecosystem with other learning resources, like infographics, podcasts, people, and networks. The future of talent development means being able to quickly and efficiently create new content in a consistent way. So, how do you structure your TD department?

Look to for ideas in the traditional TV newsroom. TV journalists must churn out stories in little to no time while maintaining high production and editorial standards. In fact, they provide an ideal model to incorporate into how TD functions are structured. In a 2017 *Training Industry* article, I argued that training leaders need to establish editorial and production standards, build robust production workflows, and actively develop the media skills of learning professionals. Since then, I want to add that we also need to focus on how we integrate standards, workflows, and skills into the broader operation of TD departments.

In many organizations, video is typically produced by one or two folks who may be video enthusiasts. Sometimes, they have an IT background, so they naturally take to the intricacies of video editing software and content management; at other times, they are amateur photographers or film buffs. They usually bear the load of the department—trainers and instructional designers come to them with requests to film and edit content. They're often overwhelmed by the pressure to craft lots of content almost overnight. It's not a sustainable approach. We need processes and systems to support them and to introduce others in the TD function to the practice so everyone can make a great video.

As tempting as it is to offer a solution, this is still a work in progress, and no one knows what best practice looks like because we're still making it up. For what it's worth, there are some things you can do to work toward editorial and production consistency, robust workflows, and solid media skills. Let's discuss them in greater detail.

Establishing Editorial and Production Consistency

If I walk past a TV playing in a public place, it doesn't take me long to figure out if it's tuned to CNN or the BBC because each network has its own visual style. All the content produced by each broadcaster is consistent—from colors to fonts to editing to transitions to screen overlays. While TD departments are not in the marketing business, I think the function needs to create a sense of brand identity for its content as well as standard templates for structuring learning.

Consistency can be achieved by creating a style guide that is followed by anyone on your team who creates training videos. Of course, style guides don't just establish branding and develop consistency. They also save time. A style guide means three or four different folks won't have to decide where to position captions, what font to use, and whether to overlay text or show it on a white or black background. They also help with reviewing content before it's signed off on. There are several things that should be included in a video style guide.

Think about the standard fonts you will use in all your productions, including the color and size. These will be different for titles and captions. Identify when captions are appropriate and specify where on the screen they should appear. If they transition, what type of transition should be used? Wipe? Fades? Cuts? Create a consistent practice for showing captions. For example, if producing a longer video in which a SME appears multiple times, do you superimpose a caption with their name every time they appear or just the first time?

Text graphics are an important tool in training videos, so adopt a consistent standard for how they appear. Should you superimpose captions on footage, or cut to a white or black screen with text on it? Should you follow an uppercase style for titles or just capitalize the beginning of sentences and proper nouns? Your choice is less important than consistently applying the style decision. If your captions have multiple lines of text, will they be left-aligned or centered?

Follow good language practices. Training videos will often be seen by people from around the world, so use inclusive language that is respectful to everyone in your audience and the different cultures they represent, whether social or national. Create a list of words to use for certain topics or activities and identify inappropriate words as well. Avoid words or phrases that work in one culture but not in others (like the baseball term "Step up to the plate"). Also, consider including guidelines on media writing, which I discussed in the video script writing section of the last chapter.

It is worth designing narrative template that producers can follow when they're planning content. For example, you'll need a template for informational videos and another for task videos. You might consider setting a standard length and consistent methods for creative repetition.

Short how-to videos that will be viewed on-demand, online may have different standards than longer versions that can last up to 10 minutes long. In addition to having a narrative template, consider creating visual templates and sequences, such as a standard five-second visual intro with text and animation.

Different people can adopt different filming styles, so establish best practices for your organization. You might consider stipulating policies on camera movement; for example, banning crash zooms or excessive pans. You might also require every video be shot on a tripod. Maybe you'll want videographers to follow the three-shot formula for task videos. Filming conventions should also include how you'll capture software on screens. Clear standards ensure everyone films in a consistent manner. Additionally, specify how to use music. For example, don't play music through the length of the video. Also, cover how to use effects and avoid video bling.

Create a policy on accessibility. Will you provide closed or open captioning? Where it is it generated—within the video player (such as Vimeo), or are captions superimposed on the video itself? A lot of video captions are generated automatically and never checked for spelling or nuance. This is usually because of time constraints, but your style guide might stipulate whether captions should be reviewed by a human (and by whom) to ensure spelling and punctuation are correct. Also, consider whether you'll include audio descriptions. In the US, the General Services Administration has created a guide on making accessible, 508-compliant videos, and Ofcom offers similar accessibility guidelines in the UK (Morin, Rubin, and Leisinger 2014; ATVOD 2012).

7 Steps to Accessible Training Videos

You produce training videos to help learners build their skills. Just as you make every effort in the traditional classroom to ensure learning is accessible, you need to do the same with video. Today's technology makes it easier to ensure videos are accessible, but you need to be intentional from the moment you start planning content. Accessibility best practices evolve with technology, research, and legal requirements, so be sure to check applicable laws and corporate guidelines to ensure your videos are compliant. Here are seven steps you can take to make videos more accessible:

▶ **Include captions.** *Captions* are text descriptions of a video's audio content that viewers can read. They are superimposed over the video and include what people or narrators in the video say, as well as descriptions of music or sound effects (Halls 2021). Captions are usually positioned in the lower third of the screen. They are helpful for people with impaired hearing or folks watching a video in noisy environments. *Open captions*, which are sometimes called *baked-in* or *burned-in captions,* are part of the video file and always on. You can't turn them off. *Closed captions* are not baked into the video file and can be turned on or off, usually by clicking the "CC" button on the video player. Most video players, such as Vimeo or YouTube, provide automatic transcriptions using AI technology. However, it's important to review and edit the captions because words are often wrong.

▶ **Offer audio descriptions.** *Audio descriptions* are spoken audio tracks that describe key visual elements in a video. They allow people who can't see the content to access information that isn't included in the audio layer. For example, a video might show an athlete resting on a step after a long run. If you're not watching the video, you wouldn't know that, so an audio description might say, "Athlete is resting on steps." *Open-audio descriptions* are baked into the video file and cannot be turned off. *Closed-audio descriptions* can be turned on or off. Audio descriptions are also helpful for people who want to consume content while engaging in another activity that prevents them from watching the video. To create audio descriptions, watch your video and note key visual elements that aren't clear from the spoken-word content. Write a script from your notes, and record your descriptions, timing each one to match the visual element. Then, add them to the audio track in the editing software. (Some video players will allow you to upload a separate track.) Use descriptive words, and avoid words like "it" or "that"; instead, use a noun that accurately describes what "it" or "that" is. You can save time by starting the script after you have completed the storyboard.

▶ **Provide a transcript.** Providing a transcript of the video is both easy and helpful. Transcripts make content more accessible to people who are deaf or blind because they can be read by the learner or a screen reader (W3C WAI n.d.). They should include the spoken-word content as well as a description of the visual elements that are key to the message and displayed on screen. Scripts can easily be turned into transcripts with a few edits, or the audio track can be loaded into an AI app that generates the transcript.

▶ **Use an accessible browser.** Most modern web browsers support accessibility with captions, audio descriptions, and transcripts. If you're embedding a video player in your content, activate all these options on the player. In addition, make sure that users can access a play and stop button; that they can pause, fast forward, or rewind the video; and that they can adjust the volume. Choose players that provide a user interface that can work without a mouse, such as with a speech interface.

▶ **Make text graphics easy to see.** Text graphics are often a key part of training videos. To be accessible, they need to be as easy to read as possible. So, restrict the number of words on the screen and make them large enough to read. Choose solid or bold sans-serif fonts that are easy to read on screen and avoid decorative cursive typefaces that aren't immediately familiar to viewers and are typically difficult to read. Put as few words on screen as possible, and avoid transitions that fly text into the screen, that zoom in or out, or that animate the text (such as creating a wobble effect). These effects make text harder to read. Many video editors hold text on screen for as long as it takes to read the text out loud twice. Avoid superimposing text over footage or other visuals that are either distracting or allow the text to bleed into the background; instead, cut to a screen with key text displayed on a one-color background, rather than superimposed over images, so it's easier to read. For example, use dark text on a light background, or vice versa.

▶ **Don't rely on colors to convey your message.** It's estimated that 300 million people around the world are colorblind (Colour Blind Awareness n.d.). Know that if you're using color to draw the eye to certain parts of an image or support a brand, your message could be lost. To avoid this, choose colors with a strong contrast so their shades are distinguishable, and consider using borders or icons to draw the eye, rather than different colors. Naturally, you'll need to work within a brand style guide, but don't use color to differentiate key information on the screen.

▶ **Be descriptive in spoken-word content.** If your video relies mostly on the visual modality to convey information and doesn't include spoken-word content, ensure captions, audio descriptions, and transcripts use descriptive words. For example, when explaining how to mix concrete, the video might show a contractor mixing gravel, cement, and water. Rather than using text that says, "Now, we mix the core ingredients," say, "Now, we mix gravel, cement, and water to make concrete." That way, if someone cannot see the mixing process, the description provides enough information so they know what's happening anyway. When reviewing your spoken-word content, look for any word that is not clear or descriptive, and replace it with one that is.

Standardizing Systems

Systems can mean many things, including the rapid video workflow I discussed in chapter 12. I want to focus on one more system here, and that's IT. I've consulted with several organizations with video teams whose members use different software programs to edit video. A client in New Jersey had three videographers producing content on Final Cut Pro, Premier Pro, and Vegas Pro. When one videographer was sick, his colleague needed to step in, but she had to learn a new editing system, which took several days. Just like you'd choose one project management system for your office, choose one editing system and stick to it.

Managing Stakeholders

If you're in a sizeable organization and tasked with creating a lot of videos for different parts of the company, the relationships you develop with stakeholders are critical. A key part of these relationships will be managing expectations. So many people who have not made a quality video simply don't understand the process or its complexity. Many think video can be produced at a moment's notice—but that just isn't the case. A two-minute video made to a standard that you'd be proud to show in a board presentation or to a group of trainees will take at least a day to plan, film, and produce.

Your job as the producer is to take a topic from a sponsor and return with a complete video package. You might be filming and editing it, or a colleague may do it for you. The most important thing you can do, apart from making the video, is keep people updated with progress reports and ensure each stakeholder understands which lane they're in so they don't step into yours. Your role goes beyond just producing video because you must also manage expectations from various stakeholders. So, let's consider the different stakeholders you may need to work with and some issues that you should be ready for:

- **SMEs.** These are the folks who ensure your video content is accurate and reflects current industry practice. A SME should be assigned to every video you produce. They bring immense knowledge and experience, but I've often found that the magic of video ignites a latent spark of creativity in them, which can turn them into backseat directors. "I think a starburst transition would be nice here." "Can we change all fonts to yellow?" Be clear that their role is content accuracy, not style or video structure. Express gratitude for their interest but draw a line between accuracy and style.

- **Sponsor.** You'll find that the person who commissions your video, often someone from within the business, will want it created faster than is possible. They typically have no idea how long it takes to produce video or what other videos you have in your pipeline. You need to educate them on the process and how long it takes. Also, let them know that each step needs to be approved by the SME—and that after this point you can't go back. Give the sponsor regular updates so they don't badger you by wanting to find out the video's progress.

- **Lawyer.** Depending on the content, a training video may need to be approved by the company's lawyer. You'll need to do some educating here too. Lawyers usually like to see scripts with words, but this is tricky because most of the message in video is conveyed visually. Discuss this with a lawyer early in the process so they understand. They may be uncomfortable not seeing a script and find it difficult to puzzle their way through a story-board, so you may need to guide them carefully and make some compromises.

- **Marketing officer.** Your video's look and feel will need to reflect (or at least support) the organization's brand style guide. And your editorial style guide should be based on the marketing style guide. However, there will be times you produce content with-out a direct line to the style guide, so you will need to consult with marketing to make sure any extra creativity does not stray out of what is considered acceptable. Liaise with the marketing department early. Let them know what you're doing so you don't have to change everything halfway through or at the end of the project. It may be a good idea to have them sign off on your style guide if you're in doubt. I've seen teams forced to undo complex video edits and even refilm footage to adopt the company brand style, which can put projects back weeks.

- **IT contact.** It's not possible in every organization, but if you can get to know your IT contact, it makes sense to have them involved in procuring hardware and software. The challenge I have seen is that IT folks are trained to support packages like Word and Outlook, but not always video and production. This helps them learn some of the peculiarities about running a video editing system on a network that is designed to for office productivity software. The more you know and consult with your IT contact, the easier it will be when your computer fails and you need help. They can also help you install nonstandard software.

- **Learning experience designer.** In some companies, the instructional or learning experience designer will ask you to create videos. In others, you may be the designer and videographer. If you're working for the designer, make sure to keep them updated on your progress. Also, if you can share assets like infographics and diagrams that are being used in other content—like asynchronous learning, job aids, or workbooks—the consistency will make everyone look better.

Defining Processes

Consider developing a series of processes that turn your operation from a cottage industry into a production powerhouse. Here are some ways to streamline your productions:

- **Service-level agreements with sponsors for every product and project.** If a division within your organization wants a video showing people how to operate a machine, create a service-level agreement with the sponsor from that division that outlines what the product is, the estimated time, and the accountabilities of key stakeholders, especially in terms of what you expect from them. This document offers a valuable opportunity to educate stakeholders on the process. It should also include a statement that addresses changes: If changes are made that affect work previously signed off on by a SME, and they impose more than a day's work (or something to that effect), the producer reserves the right to move the project to the back of the production line. This agreement should protect your time management. I've seen teams lose a week because someone didn't correctly check work that formed the basis of subsequent work.

- **Administration.** I've touched on many of these already, including the rapid video workflow, file naming conventions, and folder management policies. Also, consider how you store and share resources, such as lighting and other tools. Create a booking calendar and a process for reporting when equipment is broken. Identify who is responsible for fixing it when it breaks.
- **Copyright and permissions.** Create a process for capturing all intellectual property information. It should include collecting and filing licenses for music and stock video and images. Create release form templates to give to people who might appear in the videos so they can provide permission.
- **Sharing stock.** It is helpful to start building your own corporate stock library with videos and photographs of content you regularly use.

Developing Skills

In many cases, it's easy to identify who is a self-taught videographer and who has worked at a professional level. Professionals get in fast, film shots right the first time, and quickly move on. Self-taught folks usually take longer, faff around, and often need to correct previous work. If you work in a professional environment, like newsgathering or studio production, you don't have much leeway to fail, so your skills end up being sharp. Now that training videos are being relied upon to provide credible learning opportunities, you need to ensure that finely honed production skills are part of your repertoire.

As you produce more instructional video content, you can improve its quality by developing three important types of skills (Halls 2016a):

- **"Edutorial" skills** relate to designing content: They run parallel to core instructional design skills. These are instructional rather than media skills, and most trainers and learning experience designers will have them. They include:

- Framing learning objectives to create a focused performance outcome
- Conducting a task analysis to break down content into its constituent parts
- Creating learning pathways, which become the video structure

- **Editorial skills** relate specifically to video communication. These are the skills that traditionally belong to media producers like directors, editors, and videographers. They are not usually associated with trainers and learning experience designers but should be. They include:
  - Picture planning following visual grammar standards, such as shot sizes and camera angles, and framing shots with storyboarding
  - Narrative skills to create a narrative path that presents learning
  - Writing for video following conventions regarding phrasing, words, and writing to picture
  - Intellectual property management to acquire copyright and actor permissions

- **Production skills** are filming and editing. These are the skills that involve physically filming and editing content in a way that follows visual grammar, as well as setting up studios in offices or sets in which to film. They include:
  - Production management skills, such as drawing shot plans and scouting locations
  - Framing shots and identifying ideal lighting conditions
  - Operating a camera to get well-framed shots with crisp clear audio
  - Directing action while filming
  - Editing video following continuity editing principles

What Does All This Mean?

It used to be that you'd find one or two people in a 10- or 15-person training team who was known as "the video people." Sometimes, they had an interest in photography or were the resident IT geek. They'd usually operate on their own. Not so in tomorrow's TD department. Everyone designing learning needs a basic understanding of video production at its elemental levels. And those producing it must do so consistently as a team, following established systems and processes, and working with stakeholders in a way that ensures quality and speeds up production.

Jonathan's Guide to Training Video Buzzwords

You'll often find different words used to describe the same thing in video production in different parts of the industry and in different countries. (For example, *wide shots* and *long shots* are the same thing, and so are *lav mics* and *clip-ons*.) Here are some common buzzwords you'll often hear folks using.

180-degree rule is about where to position the camera for multiple shots in a sequence or scene. A straight line is imagined across the location's floor, and cameras face across the line for each shot.

30-degree rule is about where to position the camera for multiple shots to minimize jump cuts when editing. It suggests cameras be positioned at least 30 degrees apart on the action arc.

A

Accretion is a cognitive term referring to the process of adding new knowledge to existing schemas (Rumelhart and Norman 1978). See also *schemas* and *modes of learning*.

Animated-sequence video is a visual format. The picture is a series of illustrated moving images, like a cartoon. It is not filmed by a camera but is created in software or drawn by hand.

Asset is a technical term for individual digital elements that convey messages and are added to the timeline during editing, such as video footage, audio, and graphics. Each asset is an individual file.

Audio description is a spoken audio track describing visual elements in a video for folks who can't see the content. *Open-audio descriptions* can't be turned off, but *closed-audio descriptions* can be.

B

Bird's-eye shot is a shot angle filmed from above. Also called a helicopter or *overhead shot*, it provides visual context but should be used sparingly because it's an unnatural frame of reference for humans.

Big close-up (BCU) shot. See *extreme close-up shot*.

Boom mic. See *shotgun microphone*.

C

Captions (also called *lower thirds* or *Astons*) are text superimposed over the picture, usually in the lower right of the screen, to provide detail (such as an interviewee's name or the location). They are real-time transcriptions superimposed on the screen for accessibility. See also *closed captions* and *open captions*.

Clip-on microphone. See *lavalier microphone*.

Closed captions refer to accessible captions that can be turned on or off. See also *captions*.

Close-up shots frame a person from the top of their head down to their shoulders. It is an intimate shot that's useful for showing emotions and facial expressions.

Cognitive-load theory is an educational theory by John Sweller. It describes the effort required to manage information load during learning and offers strategies for making comprehension more efficient.

Cold shoe is a socket on cameras and camera rigs that lights, microphones, or other tools can slide into. Cold shoes have no power to run lights or condenser microphones. See also *hot shoe*.

Creative repetition is a narrative technique to provoke retrieval. Key information is repeated several times in different ways—such as a text graphic, a voice-over, and a SME interview—so viewers think it's new information.

D

Digital zoom is a software function in a camera that makes a person or object in shot appear closer or further away. Digital zoom degrades picture quality compared with optical zoom. See also *optical zoom*.

Dolly shot is a camera movement. The camera is physically moved toward or away from the action while it is recording. It gets its name from movie production—the camera is usually mounted on a dolly that sits on a track, which is then physically moved toward or away from what is being filmed.

Drone is a device that hovers and flies and is controlled by a pilot with a joystick or remote device attached to a smartphone. A camera mounted to a drone can capture bird's-eye shots and maneuverer into normally difficult areas to film. Most jurisdictions require a license to operate a drone.

E

Extreme close-up (XCU) shot frames a person's face in close proximity to the area between their mouth and forehead. It is a very unnatural shot because the camera comes in closer to their face than another person would in real life.

Extreme wide shot (XWS) captures context and is known as an *establishing shot* because it provides a visual reference for viewers about where the action takes place. It frames the shot from a distance.

Eye-level shot is a camera angle that frames a person looking across at the camera and puts both the viewer and person in shot on equal footing.

Eyeline describes where the presenter or actor on screen is looking.

F

Five-shot formula is a method for filming without a storyboard. It requires you to perform and film the action five times, placing the camera in different positions each time. This gives editors five shots to craft more engaging sequences. Generally, it includes a wide shot, a close-up of the action, a close-up of the actor's face, an over-the-shoulder shot of the action, and a creative shot; for example, a bird's-eye shot or filming the action through a window.

Fluid head is the top part of a camera tripod that the camera is attached to. Fluid is built into the head, which enables the operator to smoothly pan and tilt the camera.

FOCUS model highlights keys to effective training videos, including making content familiar, providing an outline, engaging in creative repetition, uncluttering the content, and focusing on a single objective.

Forgetting curve is a psychology model developed in the 19th century by German psychologist Herman Ebbinghaus (and replicated as recently as 2017). It suggests that people rapidly forget information that is presented to them.

Frames per second (FPS) describes how many frames are used to display movement in an image for every second of action. Each frame is slightly different, creating the illusion of movement when run together.

G

Gimbal is a camera mounting tool that creates smooth movement when filming handheld shots. It is made up of a series of weights and motors that constantly move in response the operator's movements, which holds the camera steady and ensures moving shots flow without shaking.

Graphics are visual representations of a message or data. They can include drawings, photographs, diagrams, flow charts, text, and icons.

Graphics layer is the part of the message layer model that refers to graphics. See also *graphics* and *message layers*.

H

Handheld microphone is a type of microphone that is held by the person speaking. In TV these are also known as *reporter microphones* because reporters use them when standing in front of the camera.

Hard light is a lighting term for lights that focus on a particular area of a shot, like a flashlight. Anything not under the light is left in shadow.

Headroom is a visual term that describes the space in a shot above the subject's head. Too much headroom is considered not good.

High definition (HD) refers to video shot at either 1280 x 720 or 1920 x 1080 resolution. Many learning platforms stream video at these resolutions. See also *resolution*.

High-angle shot is a camera angle where the camera looks down at the person or object. It gives viewers power because it feels like they are looking down at the person, making them seem vulnerable.

Hot shoe is a socket on the camera or camera rig that lights, microphones, or other tools can slide into. Hot shoes carry power to run lights or condenser microphones. See also *cold shoe*.

J

Jump cut is an editing term that describes a continuity break when part of an action is removed. For example, if you cut out five seconds of a shot to fit a certain amount of time, the viewer will see the action jump five seconds, which looks unnatural.

K

Key light is a lighting term that describes the primary light source in a filming environment. Outdoors, it will be the sun. Indoors, it can be a set of lights or sun coming in through a window.

L

Lavalier (lav) microphone is a small microphone used to capture speech that is clipped to clothing near a subject's mouth. It's also known as a *clip-on* or *tie-clasp mic*.

Learning formula is a model that breaks the learning process into three steps: building understanding, building memory, and applying learning to the workplace.

Learning objective is an educational statement that describes the cognitive, psychomotor, or affective task that someone will be able to perform after completing the learning experience.

Learning is the intentional process of building cognitive, psychomotor, or affective skills.

Long-term memory (LTM) is the third process in Atkinson and Shiffrin's 1968 multi-store memory model and is where long-lasting memories are encoded. No limit has been found for how much information the LTM can store. When encoded into the LTM, memories are stored indefinitely.

Long shot. See *wide shot*.

Looking space is a visual grammar term that describes the area within a frame that a subject is looking at.

Low-angle shot is a camera angle where the camera looks up at a person or object. This angle gives the person in shot power and is effective for showing a leader or a sense of authority.

M

Megapixel is a technical term for one million pixels. See also *pixels*.

Message layers is a model for categorizing elements of video as specific layers of a narrative; it includes the pictures, graphics, visual effects, spoken-word, music, and sound-effects layers. It forms the basis for the planning steps in the rapid video workflow.

Mid-close-up (MCU) shot is a shot size that frames a person from just above the elbows. There is little contextual detail in this shot; however, it emphasizes the person's emotion.

Mid-shot (MS) is a shot size that captures someone from the waist up and shows general body language within limited of context. The camera is positioned at a distance that would feel comfortable in real life.

Modes of learning is a theory that suggests people form schema by accretion (adding new information to existing schema), restructuring (building a new schema from scratch), and tuning (changing an existing schema; Rumelhart and Norman 1978). See also *schema, accretion, restructuring,* and *tuning.*

Monopod is a camera stabilization device that is like a tripod but mounted on only one leg. Monopods are easier to transport, so they are more versatile than tripods.

Multimedia principles are evidence-based principles developed by Richard Mayer from his extensive research into multimedia. They reduce cognitive load and aid learning with digital content.

Multimodal principle is a decision-making principle for choosing the appropriate modality for digital learning, assuming each modality has its own strengths and weaknesses for different types of content.

Music layer refers to the use of music within the message layer to affect mood and emotion, influence energy level, and provide situational context.

O

Open captions are captions that are displayed in the video file and cannot be turned off. See also *captions.*

Optical zoom is a series of physical lenses and mechanical elements in a camera that are manipulated to adjust focal length, which allows the image to appear closer or further away. Unlike digital zoom, it does not lead to a degradation of picture quality. See also *digital zoom.*

Optical-sequence video is a visual format. Content is filmed by a camera in multiple shots and cut into a sequence to tell a story or convey a message. The pictures, not a narrator or presenter, carry the bulk of the message.

P

Personas are fictional characters who represent typical audience members. Producers use personas to identify ways to make video elements more relevant to viewers' language, experiences, and interests.

Picture is a general term used to describe anything seen in a video, such as video footage, graphics, animation, or special effects. It comes from the traditional term *motion picture*. Pictures are the foundational building block of engaging video and carry the bulk of the message.

Picture layer is the foundation of the message layer model. It includes shots learners see in the video, which are filmed and edited together following the rules of visual grammar. See also *picture* and *message layers*.

Pixels is the technical term for the small, square dots that images are broken down into. Pixels display three colors—red, green, and blue. The higher number of pixels in an image (which is generally measured by square inch), the more detail the image has. The term combines *picture* (pix) and *elements* (els).

Point-of-view (POV) is a filming style used by videographers who want to film life through the eyes of the protagonist, rather than construct a narrative from a disinterested third-person perspective.

Point-of-view (POV) camera is a type of camera designed to capture footage from a person's perspective. The most common POV camera is the GoPro. Another POV camera is a secret camera, which may be hidden in a button, and is used by investigative journalists.

Principle of change assumes people, especially their eyes, are drawn to anything that changes. It explains why video (moving pictures) draws the eye. This principle applies to every element of video (and media), which is why subtly changing music, pace, shots, sound effects, and other elements all keep viewers engaged.

Principle of incompleteness asserts that people are drawn to incomplete things because we crave a sense of homeostasis. This principle is at the heart of visual elements like the rule of thirds and shot changes, as well as in narrative elements like suspense, asymmetry, and conflict.

Q

Quick-release plate is the detachable mount on a tripod that cameras are screwed into. It is easily removed so the camera operator can carry the tripod and camera separately.

R

Resolution is a technical term for picture quality describing how many pixels are used to display the image. The higher the pixel count, the better the picture quality. Resolution is described in terms of vertical versus horizontal pixels, such as 1920 x 1080. See also *high definition* and *standard definition*.

Restructuring is the intellectual process of building new schemas (Rumelhart and Norman 1978). See also *schemas* and *modes of learning*.

Retrieval refers to the cognitive process of accessing information from the LTM. Retrieval practice drives the formation of memory. See also *working memory* and *long-term memory*.

Rough cut is an editing term for the initial edit that positions assets in order—before they are polished for final rendering—so producers can have a general idea of how the video will play.

Rule of thirds is a visual term for describing the compositional principle of framing important elements in a shot at the intersection of the three lines formed by dividing the screen into three sections.

S

SAFA model is a workflow designed to speed up video editing and make it consistent. It has four steps: sequence (assemble shots in sequence as a rough cut), accuracy (check the accuracy of content and pictures), flow (finetune the rough edit so it conforms to acceptable visual grammar), and approve (have a SME review and approve the final video).

Scene is a film term for a collection of sequences that show a series of action or events. Scenes are like paragraphs of sentences (sequences).

Schema is a cognitive term for the mental models that a person constructs in their mind to make sense of the world. Schemas include facts, concepts, and experiences. See also *modes of learning*.

Segmenting is a cognitive term for breaking longer content into shorter chunks to make it easier to learn.

Sensor is the silicon component inside a digital camera that determines how much light to let in and turns what is being filmed into an electrical signal.

Sequence is a film term for a series of shots that show an action in a continuous flowing manner. A sequence is like a sentence that shows, rather than tells, an action.

Shot is a film term for the action or event recorded on a camera between pressing record and stop. Shots make up sequences of action and are analogous to words in a sentence.

Shotgun microphone is a long cylindrically shaped microphone that is more sensitive to sounds in front of it than by its side. Musicians call it a *boom mic*.

Shot plan is a production tool for scheduling which shots are filmed, at what time, in what order, and with what props and costumes.

Short-term memory (STM) is a cognitive term for where memories are processed. It originated from Atkinson and Shiffrin's 1968 multistore model and was later challenged by Baddeley and Hitch's understanding of working memory.

Signaling is a cognitive term for using visual elements like text or graphics to highlight a key area in the frame that carries important information.

Soft light is a lighting term for light that wraps around a person, object, or location and minimizes harsh shadows. Fluorescent lights provide soft lighting. In TV production, professionals place a soft box around the lights to diffuse them.

Sound effects are audio recordings of a noise or part of a noise—such as a car door slamming shut or a clap of thunder—that are added to the audio soundtrack to add realism to the video.

Sound-effects layer is part of the message layer model that refers to sound effects. See also *sound effects* and *message layers.*

Spirit level is the water-filled vial with a bubble that's built into a tripod to show when the tripod is perfectly horizontal. (The bubble rests in the center of the vial.) This helps videographers adjust the tripod to ensure the camera is level.

Spoken word is a narrative term that refers to content in a video featuring people talking. It includes monologues (someone speaking to camera), dialogues (two people talking, such as in an interview), and commentary (narration or a voice-over).

Spoken-word layer is the part of the message layer model that refers to spoken-word content and is about writing to picture instead of following conventional written grammar. See also *spoken word* and *message layers.*

Stabilization is a technical term for making video look steady. It is physically achieved by mounting the camera on a tripod or using a stabilization device like a gimbal. It can also be achieved through the stabilization software built into the camera or included in the editing software.

Standard definition (SD) is a technical term that refers to video filmed at 720 x 480 pixels. This was the standard definition used on terrestrial (or over-the-air) TV before widescreen and high definition. See also *resolution.*

Storyboard is a film term for the visual representation of the shots being filmed in a sequence or scene. It includes camera direction and sometimes a dialogue summary. It's often sketched with stick figures.

T

Talking-head video is a visual format centered on one person talking to the camera. It may cut to graphics or B-roll, but the message is carried by the presenter and what they say.

Text graphic is a standalone graphic asset that is made up primarily of text. It does not refer to captions, which are superimposed over pictures. Text generally appears on a blank background.

Three-point lighting is a lighting term that describes a method for lighting a set using three lights: a key light, a fill light, and a back light.

Three-shot formula is a method for filming without a storyboard. It requires you to perform and film the action three times, placing the camera in different positions each time, which gives the editor three shots to work with to craft more engaging sequences. Generally, it includes a wide shot of the action, a close-up of the task, and a mid-shot of the action.

Tie-clasp microphone. See *lavalier microphone.*

Timeline is a technical term for the area of editing software where assets are positioned when editing.

Transition is an editing term for the action of moving from one shot to another. The most common transition used in TV is the cut. Most transitions fall into one of four broader categories: the cut, dissolve, wipe, or fade.

Tripod is a three-legged device for mounting cameras to ensure steady shots. Video tripods have a fluid head that supports the camera.

Tuning is a cognitive term for the intellectual process of modifying existing schemas to meet needs for new tasks or knowledge (Rumelhart and Norman 1978). See also *schemas* and *modes of learning.*

U

Ultra-high frequency (UHF) is part of the radio spectrum. Many wireless microphones transmit on UHF, which is highly effective indoors and in crowded areas.

V

Very-high frequency (VHF) is part of the radio spectrum. It's beneficial in wide open spaces but has difficulty penetrating things, so it's less effective if concrete or metal objects are in the way. Many wireless

microphones transmit on VHF, although it's prone to more distur-
bance than UHF.

Very long shot (VLS). See *extreme wide shot.*

Visual effects are manipulations that are applied to assets to help them
better portray a message. They include transitions (such as cut or
dissolve), manipulations (such as slow motion or freeze frame), and
filters (such as transforming a color into monochrome).

Visual-effects layer is part of the message layer model that refers to visual effects. See also *visual effects* and *message layers.*

Voice-over is spoken-word content that is recorded over a music track or
atmosphere and provides information that a picture can't. Normally,
the volume of the music or atmosphere is lowered so the voice-over
is easy to hear.

W

Weeding is a cognitive term for the process of removing content
elements that do not support the learning objective.

Wide shot (WS) shows the context of a person from head to toe. This shot
is useful for showing action and body language.

WIIFM is an abbreviation for the phrase "What's in it for me?" It's used to
describe key benefits for an individual.

WIIFO is an abbreviation for the phrase "What's in it for the organization?" It's used to describe key benefits for an organization.

Windsock is a textile or sponge form that fits over a microphone and is
used to reduce the sound of wind when recording outdoors. It's also
used indoors on a reporter's microphone to reduce breathing noise
and marginally minimize plosives.

Working memory (WM) is a cognitive term for where information is
processed in the brain. It was proposed by Baddeley and Hitch to
replace the short-term memory concept in Atkinson and Shiffrin's
1968 multi-store model.

References

Adavelli, M. 2023. "24 Noteworthy Video Consumption Statistics [2023 Edition]." Techjury Blog, July 5. techjury.net/blog/video-consumption -statistics/#gref.

Atkinson, R.C., and R.M. Shiffrin. 1968. "Human Memory: A Proposed System and Its Control Processes." In *The Psychology of Learning and Motivation*, Vol. 2, edited by K.W. Spence and J.T. Spence, 89–195. New York: Academic Press.

ATVOD (The Authority for Television on Demand). 2012. "Video on Demand Access Services: Best Practice Guidelines for Service Providers." Ofcom. ofcom.org.uk/__data/assets/pdf_file/0018/82242 /access_services_best_practice_guidelines_final_120912.pdf.

Baddeley, A.D., and G.J. Hitch. 1974. "Working Memory." In *The Psychology of Learning and Motivation: Advances in Research and Theory*, Vol. 8, edited by G.H. Bower. New York: Academic Press.

Bartlett, F. (1932) 1995. *Remembering: A Study in Experimental and Social Psychology*, 2nd ed. New York: University Press.

Bloom, B.S., M.D. Englehart, E.J. Furst, W.H. Hill, and D. Krathwohl. 1956. *Taxonomy of Educational Objectives*. The Classification of Educational Goals. Handbook 1: Cognitive Domain. New York: Longman.

Bowen, C.J., and R. Thompson. 2013a. *Grammar of the Edit*, 3rd ed. Burlington, MA: Focal Press.

Bowen, C.J., and R. Thompson. 2013b. *Grammar of the Shot*, 3rd ed. Burlington, MA: Focal Press.

Brady, F. 1998. "A Theoretical and Empirical Review of the Contextual Interference Effect and the Learning of Motor Skills." *Quest (National Association for Kinesiology in Higher Education)* 50(3): 266–293.

Campbell, M. 2022. "21st-Century Media Skills: Put Learning Where the Work Is." Chapter 17 in *ATD's Handbook for Training and Talent Development*, edited by E. Biech. Alexandria, VA: ATD Press.

Clapp, A., and L. Devine. 2023. "Tap Memory Structures for Learning Success." *TD at Work*. Alexandria, VA: ATD Press.

Colour Blind Awareness. n.d. "About Colour Blindness." Colour Blind Awareness. colourblindawareness.org/colour-blindness.

Cowan, N. 2010. "The Magical Mystery Four: How Is Working Memory Capacity Limited, and Why?" *Current Directions in Psychological Science* 19(1): 51–57. doi.org/10.1177/0963721409359277.

Dash, S., U. Kamath, G. Rao, J. Prakash, and S. Mishra. 2016. "Audio–Visual Aid in Teaching 'Fatty Liver.'" *Biochemistry and Molecular Biology Education* 44:241–245. doi.org/10.1002/bmb.20935.

Ebbinghaus, H. (1885) 1913. *Memory: A Contribution to Experimental Psychology*. Translated by H.A. Ruger and C.E. Bussenius. New York: Teachers College.

Ebbinghaus, H. (1885) 1962. *Memory: A Contribution to Experimental Psychology*. New York: Dover.

Foshay, W.R. 2008. "Research in Learning: What We Know for Sure." Chapter 9 in *ASTD Handbook for Workplace Learning Professionals*, edited by E. Biech. Alexandria, VA: ASTD Press.

Frechette, C. 2012. "How Journalists Can Improve Video Stories With Shot Sequences." Poynter, August 13. poynter.org/newsletters/2012/how-journalists-can-improve-video-stories-with-shot-sequences.

Gagne, R. 1965. *Conditions of Learning*. New York: Holt, Rinehart, and Winston.

Guo, P.J., J. Kim, and R. Rubin. 2014. "How Video Production Affects Student Engagement: An Empirical Study of MOOC Videos." *Proceedings of the First ACM Conference on Learning @ Scale Conference*, March:41–50. doi.org/10.1145/2556325.2566239.

Halls, J. 2012. *Rapid Video Development for Trainers*. Alexandria, VA: ATD Press.

Halls, J. 2015. *Video Script Writing: How to Writer Better Scripts for Your Video*. Clifton, VA: Talkshow Media.

Halls, J. 2016a. "Media Mastery." *TD*, November.

Halls, J. 2016b. *Rapid Media Development for Trainers*. Alexandria, VA: ATD Press.

Halls, J. 2016c. "Video: The Change Principle." ATD Blog, April 19. td.org /atd-blog/video-the-change-principle.

Halls, J. 2017. "Tomorrow's Training Departments Should Look Like Newsrooms." *Training Industry*, July 19. trainingindustry.com /articles/content-development/tomorrows-training-departments -should-look-like-newsrooms.

Halls, J. 2019. *Confessions of a Corporate Trainer: An Insider Tells All*. Alexandria, VA: ATD Press.

Halls, J. 2021. *How Organizations Are Using Video*. Santa Rosa, CA: The Learning Guild.

Hilliard, R.L. 2011. *Writing for Television, Radio and New Media*, 10th ed. Stamford, CT: Cengage Learning.

IBM. n.d. "What Is a Workflow?" IBM. ibm.com/topics/workflow.

Ibrahim, M., P. Antonenko, C. Greenwood, and D. Wheeler. 2012. "Effects of Segmenting, Signaling, and Weeding on Learning From Educational Video." *Learning, Media, and Technology* 37(3): 220–235. doi.org /10.1080/17439884.2011.585993.

Jones, K.M. 2013. "Silent Hitchcock." *Wall Street Journal*, June 26. wsj.com /articles/SB10001424127887323683504578565833917463370.

Keast, G. 2015. *The Art of the Cut: Editing Concepts Every Filmmaker Should Know*. Honolulu: Kahala Press.

Knowles, M.S., E.F. Holton III, and R.A. Swanson. 2005. *The Adult Learner: The Definitive Classic in Adult Education and Human Resource Development*, 6th ed. Burlington, MA: Elsevier.

Krathwohl, D.R., B.S. Bloom, and B.B. Masia. 1964. *Taxonomy of Educational Objectives: The Classification of Educational Goals: Handbook II: Affective Domain*. New York: David McKay Company.

Liew, T.W., S. Tan, T.M. Tan, and S.N. Kew. 2020. "Does Speaker's Voice Enthusiasm Affect Social Cue, Cognitive Load and Transfer in Multimedia Learning?" *Information and Learning Sciences* 121:117–135. doi.org/10.1108/ILS-11-2019-0124.

Lin, F.R., J.K. Niparko, and L. Ferrucci. 2011. "Hearing Loss Prevalence in the United States." *Archives of Internal Medicine* 171(20): 1851–1852. doi: 10.1001/archinternmed.2011.506.

Lovell, O. 2020. *Sweller's Cognitive Load Theory in Action*. Woodbridge, England: John Catt Educational.

Mager, R. 1997. *Preparing Instructional Objectives: A Critical Tool in the Development of Effective Instruction*, 3rd ed. Atlanta: Center for Effective Performance.

Malmberg, K.J., J.G.W. Raaijmakers, and R.M. Shiffrin. 2019. "50 Years of Research Sparked by Atkinson and Shiffrin (1968)." *Memory & Cognition* 47:561–574. doi.org/10.3758/s13421-019-00896-7.

Martina, A.R., A. Vincent, and N. Rummel. 2013. "Interleaved Practice in Multi-Dimensional Learning Tasks: Which Dimension Should We Interleave?" *Learning and Instruction* 23:98–114.

Mayer, R.E. 2020. *Multimedia Learning*, 3rd ed. New York: Cambridge University Press.

Mercado, G. 2011. *The Filmmaker's Eye: Learning (and Breaking) the Rules of Cinematic Composition*. Burlington, MA: Focal Press.

Morin, G., J. Rubin, and R. Leisinger. 2014. "508 Accessible Videos—Why (and How) to Make Them." Digital.gov, June 30. digital.gov/2014/06/30/508-accessible-videos-why-and-how-to-make-them.

Murch, W. 2001. *In the Blink of an Eye*, 2nd ed. West Hollywood, CA: Silman-James Press.

Oberlo. n.d. "Online Video Consumption Statistics." Oberlo. oberlo.com/statistics/online-video-consumption-statistics.

Porter, S. 2015. *To MOOC or Not to MOOC: How Can Online Learning Help to Build the Future of Higher Education?* Waltham, MA: Chandos Publishing.

Ray, V. 2003. *The Television News Handbook: An Insider's Guide to Being a Great Broadcast Journalist.* London: Pan McMillan.

Rumelhart, D. 1980. "Schemata: The Building Blocks of Cognition." In *Theoretical Issues in Reading Comprehension: Perspectives From Cognitive Psychology, Linguistics, Artificial Intelligence, and Education*, edited by R.J. Spiro, B.C. Bruce, and W.F. Brewer. Hillsdale, NJ: Lawrence Erlbaum Associates.

Rumelhart, D., and D. Norman. 1978. "Accretion, Tuning, and Restructuring: Three Modes of Learning." In *Semantic Factors in Cognition*, edited by J.W. Cotton and R. Klatzky. Hillsdale, NJ: Lawrence Erlbaum Associates.

Schrader, C., M. Reichelt, and S. Zander. 2018. "The Effect of the Personalization Principle on Multimedia Learning: The Role of Student Individual Interests as a Predictor." *Educational Technology Research and Development* 66:1387–1397. doi.org/10.1007/s11423-018-9588-8.

Shepherd, J. 2023. "30 Vital Video Marketing Statistics You Need to Know in 2023." Social Shepherd Blog, May 15. thesocialshepherd.com/blog/video-marketing-statistics.

W3C WAI (World Wide Web Consortium Web Accessibility Initiative). n.d. "Making Audio and Video Media Accessible." w3.org/WAI/media/av.

Index

camera movement, 108–09
camera position
    30-degree rule, 113–14
    180-degree rule, 112–13
    and the viewer, 155–56
camera stabilizers
    fluid heads, 145
    gimbals, 147, 163
    importance of, 144, 159
    phone rigs, 146, 161
    tripods and monopods, 144–46,
        159–62
    without tools, 163–65
Camtasia video editor, 42, 43, 103,
    174, 184
Canva graphic design platform, 43
captions, 63, 123, 129, 218–19, 225–27
chroma key ("green screen"), 64
close-up (CU) shot, 80, 81
clothing and uniforms, 47
cognitive psychology
    cognitive load research, 38
    cognitive load theory, 38
    the "cognitive revolution" of the
        1950s and 1960s, 21–22
cold shoe, 146, 148–49
color choices, 123–24, 228–29
composition and the rule of thirds,
    84–86, 166
consistency, editorial and production,
    224–26, 229–30
content, video
    breaking down the content, 202–03
    FOCUS model, 46–53
    uncluttering, 51–52
    writing a treatment, 70
continuity editing, 178–80
conversational tone, 33
cut (editing transition), 181
cutting on the action, 182

D

demographics, viewer, 48–49
describer video template, 94–96
developments in the ability to create
    videos
    editing and templating systems, 16
    file size, 15

filming with smartphones, 15
    style changes, 16
devices and viewing locations, 14,
    204–05
diagrams, 118–19
directional flow of action, matching
    the, 111
dissolve (editing transition), 181
drones, 152–53

E

Ebbinghaus, Herman, 26
editing
    continuity editing, 178–80
    cutting on the action, 182
    developing editorial skills, 234
    the editing interface, 184–86
    filming extra footage to allow
        for, 170
    piano playing example, 179–80
    processing power demands,
        183, 185
    repackaging existing video into
        small chunks, 101–03
    rough cut, 188
    software, 138–39, 183–86
    time requirements for editing and
        production, 9, 67, 102, 198, 203
    transitions, 63–64, 181
    using AI tools, 16, 103
    woodworking analogy, 177–78
the editing process
    1—Sequence, 187–88
    2—Accuracy, 187, 188
    3—Flow, 187, 188–89
    4—Approve, 187, 189
    publishing analogy, 186–87
educational videos
    additional training tools to support
        engagement, 29
    benefits of, 3
    drawbacks of, 28–29
    statistics, vii–viii
edutorial skills, 233–34
effects, 109–10, 182–83
elements of a shot
    background, 107
    effects, 109–10

About the Author

Jonathan Halls's popular workshops and boot camps on how to create training videos have been enjoyed by thousands of learning professionals in hundreds of organizations around the world. And his bestselling 2012 book, *Rapid Video Development for Trainers*, has been used by learning designers to develop workflows and techniques that incorporate video into their learning design processes.

Based in the Washington, DC, area, Jonathan runs a talent development practice and is an adjunct professor at George Washington University. His 30 years of experience in talent development spans 25 countries and includes time as a learning executive at the BBC (where he ran the corporation's prestigious television, radio operations, and digital media training) and later providing talent development consulting to newspapers around Europe for digital transformation projects. Jonathan's career started in media in the 1990s as a talk show host with a short stint in corporate communications. Today, he runs workshops in change management, evidence-based train-the-trainer programs, talent strategy, and how to make training videos.

Jonathan has been active with ATD for two decades, most recently as a member of ATD's Talent Development Capability Model advisory committee and the *TDBoK Guide* review advisory board. He's a popular keynote speaker on topics across talent development and author of multiple books, including the award-winning *Confessions of a Corporate*

Trainer: An Insider Tells All (2019), *Rapid Media for Trainers* (2016), *Rapid Video Development for Trainers* (2012), and *Video Script Writing* (2014), as well as the *Infoline* "Memory and Cognition in Learning" (2014). He is also a contributing author to several books, including *ASTD Handbook: The Definitive Reference for Training and Development* (2014) and *ATD's Handbook for Training and Talent Development* (2022). In addition, he has written for publications like *TD* and *Learning Solutions*. He has a master's and a bachelor's in adult education.

Connect with Jonathan at linkedin.com/in/jonathanhalls. Learn more about his other books and programs and access available tools at jonathanhalls.com.

About ATD

The Association for Talent Development (ATD) is the world's largest association dedicated to those who develop talent in organizations. Serving a global community of members, customers, and international business partners in more than 100 countries, ATD champions the importance of learning and training by setting standards for the talent development profession.

Our customers and members work in public and private organizations in every industry sector. Since ATD was founded in 1943, the talent development field has expanded significantly to meet the needs of global businesses and emerging industries. Through the Talent Development Capability Model, education courses, certifications and credentials, memberships, industry-leading events, research, and publications, we help talent development professionals build their personal, professional, and organizational capabilities to meet new business demands with maximum impact and effectiveness.

One of the cornerstones of ATD's intellectual foundation, ATD Press offers insightful and practical information on talent development, training, and professional growth. ATD Press publications are written by industry thought leaders and offer anyone who works with adult learners the best practices, academic theory, and guidance necessary to move the profession forward.

We invite you to join our community. Learn more at **TD.org**.